Teaching ELLs to Read

In this essential book from ELL expert Paul Boyd-Batstone, you'll find out how to teach reading while keeping in mind the unique needs of English language learners. You'll learn best practices and differentiated strategies for each domain of the Common Core Foundational Reading Skills, including print concepts, phonological awareness, phonics and word recognition, and fluency.

Topics covered include:

- ideas for using contextual support to help ELLs climb the staircase of complexity;
- how to teach print concepts, such as noting word separation and using punctuation;
- strategies for teaching phonological awareness, including distinguishing vowel sounds and blending sounds;
- ways to teach phonics and word recognition using informational and literary texts; and
- exemplary ideas for teaching fluency, such as through poetry, drama, and digital media.

The book is filled with ready-to-use activities and complete lesson plans that address selected Common Core State Standards (CCSS) performance tasks at each grade level. These lesson plans demonstrate how to differentiate instruction based on your ELLs' reading levels. The book also includes performance-level descriptors, rubrics, and templates, available for free download from our website at www.routledge.com/books/details/9781138017696.

Paul Boyd-Batstone, PhD, is a professor and chair of the Department of Teacher Education at California State University, Long Beach. He is also editor of the *California Reader*, the practitioner journal for the California Reading Association.

Teaching ELLs to Read

Strategies to Meet the Common Core, K–5

Paul Boyd-Batstone

Routledge
Taylor & Francis Group

NEW YORK AND LONDON

First published 2015
by Routledge
711 Third Avenue, New York, NY 10017

and by Routledge
2 Park Square, Milton Park, Abingdon, Oxon, OX14 4RN

Routledge is an imprint of the Taylor & Francis Group, an informa business

© 2015 Taylor & Francis

The right of Paul Boyd-Batstone to be identified as author of this work
has been asserted by him in accordance with sections 77 and 78 of the
Copyright, Designs and Patents Act 1988.

Library of Congress Cataloging-in-Publication Data
Boyd-Batstone, Paul.
    Teaching ELLs to read : strategies to meet the common core, k–5 /
Paul Boyd-Batstone.
        pages cm
    Includes bibliographical references.
  1. English language—Study and teaching (Elementary)—
Foreign speakers.   2. English language—Study and teaching
(Elementary)—United States.   3. Second language acquisition—
United States.   4. Educational tests and measurements—United
States.   I. Title.
    PE1128.A2B655   2015
    372.4—dc23
    2014037482

ISBN: 978-1-138-01768-9 (hbk)
ISBN: 978-1-138-01769-6 (pbk)
ISBN: 978-1-315-78027-6 (ebk)

Typeset in Palatino
by Apex CoVantage, LLC

Printed and bound in the United States of America by Publishers Graphics,
LLC on sustainably sourced paper.

To write a book is one thing; but to see my daughter become an accomplished woman with a caring heart, a keen mind, and an eye for beauty is a work of wonder.

This book is dedicated to Kathryn René Boyd-Batstone, my girl.

Contents

eResources

Many of the tools in this book can be downloaded and printed for classroom use. You can access these downloads by visiting the book product page on our website: www.routledge.com/books/details/9781138017696. Then click on the tab that says "eResources," and select the files. They will download to your computer.

eResources

.

1

Introduction
Teaching English Language Learners to Read

Reading is a remarkable process. It begins with learning to read non-verbal clues such as facial expressions and tone of voice; it develops with listening to stories, understanding ideas and directions, and making sense of illustrations. Foundational skills in reading involve grasping concepts about the form and structure of print; discerning and articulating the phonology of the language in meaningful ways; hearing and seeing how letters combine to make words; and purposefully reading with accuracy, pacing, and expression. Building a strong foundation for reading with English language learners (ELLs) involves additional supports with a strong focus on developing meaning. It also requires that teachers bring linguistic and cultural insights into their reading instruction.

ELLs present unique instructional challenges to teaching reading, which confront conventional notions of practice, even at the foundational skills level. This book specifically addresses teaching ELLs to read at the foundational level. More accurately, this book addresses how to prepare ELLs to meet the goals established by the Common Core State Standards (CCSS, 2010) for Foundational Skills in Reading. Foundational Skills in Reading, according to the CCSS, encompass four areas, or domains, in the English language arts. They are: Concepts about Print, Phonological Awareness, Phonics and Word Recognition, and Fluency. These skills are based on established research (August & Shanahan, 2006; Griffin, Burns, & Snow, 1998; NRP, 2000). They lay the foundation for reading instruction for kindergarten through 5th grade. These foundational skills support the other reading standards for literature and informational texts, K–12th grade. The CCSS, however, did not prescribe how to teach ELLs to read. That remarkable task was given back to teachers like you.

The Common Core provided a set of goals; but did not map out the pathway for ELLs to learn to read. The Common Core established grade level expectations; but did not propose instructional strategies to teach ELLs to read. Rightfully so, the framers of CCSS recognized the professionalism and grounded knowledge that teachers bring to the classroom setting. However, one major challenge for classroom teachers today is that one in four students in classrooms across the country are ELLs, and that ratio is much higher in urban areas of the United States. Another challenge is that language development for ELLs does not strictly adhere to a grade leveled progression, which is how the CCSS has been structured. Meeting these challenges requires teachers to interpret and apply CCSS-based teaching of reading in thoughtful and innovative ways to benefit ELLs.

Establishing a strong foundation for reading so that ELLs can comprehend more complex texts requires a range of supports. But as schools are finding out, the more they provide supports for ELLs to learn, the greater the benefit to all learners. The supports begin in the classroom with teachers, who are equipped by administrative systems with ample resources. When teachers gain insight about language development and the range of factors that influence teaching and learning of ELLs, all their students benefit. Having quality sets of literary and informational texts, rich supplies of materials like realia and visuals, and equal access to curriculum and technology can only benefit the entire educational community. Many of the strategies in this book that are particularly effective for ELLs have broad application to all students.

Who Is This Book for?

CCSS FAQ: Do standards tell teachers how to teach?

Teachers know best about what works in the classroom. That is why these standards establish what students need to learn, but do not dictate how teachers should teach. Instead, schools and teachers decide how best to help students reach the standards. (CCSS, 2010, retrieved from www.corestandards.org/about-the-standards/frequently-asked-questions/)

Classroom Teachers. The primary audience of this book is teachers who teach ELLs to read, grades K–5, in alignment with CCSS Foundational Reading

Skills. This book is for teachers who are charged with developing print concepts in early grades, and teachers at any grade who have students whose concept of print does not use English script. This book is for teachers who develop phonological awareness of consonants and vowels, syllables, and all phonemes; and for teachers whose students mix up where a floating -*s* attaches in the phrases ". . . the girl run*s* or the girl*s* run . . .". This book is for K–5 teachers, and teachers at higher grade levels, whose students need help with sound-symbol relationships and word recognition. Learning is recursive, so that when new content and vocabulary are introduced, teachers return to foundational skills to help students decode new words and complex terminology. Many of the same decoding strategies apply to learning and array of words such as *code, zip-code, codex, codify, codification*, and *decodable*. This book is for teachers whose ELLs' reading fluency suffers because they remain at the level of deciphering individual words, rather than reading for comprehension of ideas with accuracy, pacing, and expression.

Literacy Coaches and ELL Specialists. The reading field has gone through a paradigm shift with the advent of the Common Core. As school districts work to implement the goals of CCSS, they are relying heavily on Literacy Coaches and ELL Specialists to interpret the standards, develop appropriate instructional experiences, and disseminate effective approaches directly to classroom teachers. Foundational Skills in Reading are now positioned alongside standards for literary and informational texts. There is a stronger emphasis on integrating foundational reading skills into performance tasks that call for higher-level thinking and habits of mind that support college readiness. As students are developing their foundational skills, they are also asked to explore previously unknown words, compare and contrast ideas, dig into informational texts for details, and argue a point of view. The activities and lesson plans provided in this book are exemplars that can be adapted to your particular school context. The explanations of linguistic and culturally responsive instruction are designed to provide insight into your teaching.

School Administrators. School administrators will find this book resourceful as they observe and mentor classroom teachers of ELLs. It will foster insight into why a teacher of ELLs might begin, for example, a fluency lesson with vocabulary building. The formative assessment tools suggested in this book will help administrators recognize, at a glance, at what level a student is demonstrating concepts of print or phonological awareness. Understanding these levels will help administrators speak clearly with parents about their children's instructional needs. Administrators will find helpful examples for lesson planning and evaluating the alignment of a lesson plan with CCSS. I am especially hopeful that administrators will learn from this book how best to support classroom teachers with networks for teaming, time for assessment conversations and sharing of ideas, ample sets of materials, and access to quality resources and appropriate technology. Research tells us very clearly (August and Shanahan, 2006) that, despite the heroic efforts of individual teachers, effective instruction of ELLs requires systems of support designed to foster learning within an educational community. It is the administrators' calling to develop those systems of support for teachers of ELLs.

Informed Practitioners. This book is for the informed practitioner who works with ELLs. Educational researchers like Burkhardt and Schoenfeld (2003) remind us that if our work is not useful and applicable to classroom settings, it is not rigorous. In this book, the recommended strategies and activities are practitioner-focused. They are grounded in established theory, vetted research, and are ready for current practice. Although the stance of this book is to align instruction with CCSS, at times I step back to take a critical look at the Common Core, particularly where the CCSS is based more on assumptions than on theory, research, and practice. The recommendations in these pages are readily applicable for classroom instruction, including differentiated applications by performance-level and grade-level; they are backed with exemplars including complete lesson plans in full alignment with CCSS.

Conceptual Approach

Integrated and Interconnected. There is an underlying conceptual approach, central to the English Language Arts (ELA) Common Core State Standards (CCSS), that impacts how we teach all students to read—a common foundation to teaching and learning. The ELA-CCSS takes an integrated and interconnected approach to literacy development. Each domain of the CCSS, including Foundational Skills in Reading, does not stand alone, to be taught in isolation, or at a separate time, or only in a specific subject area. Just as with the other domains of the ELA-CCSS, Foundational Skills in Reading apply across the curriculum, as it should be for teaching ELLs to read. For example, content area instructors will find foundational skills to be highly applicable to introducing new concepts with disciplinary specific vocabulary. Further, every discipline works to develop fluency in their content area. Therefore, the purpose of this book is to show how to integrate reading instruction of CCSS foundational skills for ELLs, K–5. This book will take an integrated and interconnected approach to teaching with special attention to the instructional factors unique to teaching ELLs to read.

Context Supports Complexity. Another feature of this book is that the recommended strategies and activities are designed to prepare ELLs to meet the foundational standards. This implies, as in the first paragraph of this chapter, that teaching ELLs to read requires building comprehension first before teaching the foundational skills. At first glance, it might appear to be counter-intuitive, we see foundational skills as the beginning point of reading instruction; however, the metaphor I am applying is to prepare the ground before laying the foundation. The instructional groundwork is to first provide meaningful context (Boyd-Batstone, 2006, 2013; Cummins, 1994) with visuals, real objects, primary language support, experiences, and exemplars to develop comprehension before introducing the text. Keep in mind that a text is comprised of abstract letters, words, and paragraphs that at first look to an ELL may be quite meaningless. Providing contextual understanding prepares the ground to lay foundational skills, which in turn becomes a very efficient way to teach ELLs to read. The refrain that you will hear repeated in these pages is *context supports complexity*.

Differentiated Instruction. This book will take a differentiated approach to instruction because no two ELLs are alike. For example, two newly arrived immigrants from the same country and same language group may have very different socio-economic backgrounds, educational attainment, and levels of literacy in their home language. Sibling ELLs may favor different cognitive processes and modalities of learning. Or some ELLs in your classroom may speak a language that does not use the same script as in English. These are significant factors that need to be addressed in order to meet the foundational expectations of the Common Core.

There are many ways to differentiate instruction. For example, in my previous book, *Helping English language learners meet the Common Core: Assessment and instructional strategies, K–12* (Boyd-Batstone, 2013), I focused on differentiating instruction according to oral language development to address CCSS for Listening and Speaking. With this current book, we will be differentiating instruction according to performance level descriptors (PLDs) of the four domains of the Foundational Skills in Reading: Print Concepts, Phonological Awareness, Phonics and Word Recognition, and Fluency.

The CCSS encourages teachers to develop formative assessment tools to inform differentiated instruction. Table 1.1 shows one such tool that I developed for this book. I've titled it *Foundational Reading Performance Levels*. Each domain is provided with three different PLDs that help the teacher identify the level of instruction for appropriate differentiation. These *Foundational Reading Skill Levels* are not designed as a comprehensive assessment of reading skills, rather, they provide the classroom teacher with a descriptive handle to identify and apply appropriate instruction.

The *Foundational Reading Performance Levels* are numbered 1, 2, or 3. Performance level 3 is the academic learning goal: to function at grade level expectations according to the CCSS Anchor Standard for each of the four domains

Table 1.1 Foundational Reading Performance Levels

Foundational Reading Skills/ Performance Level Descriptors (PLDs)	Performance Level 1 Undeveloped foundational skills	Performance Level 2 Developing grade level foundational skills	Performance Level 3 Grade level foundational skills
Print Concepts	Does not recognize print in English as significant. Does not track words from left to right. Names a few to no letters in the alphabet. No use of punctuation.	Sees words as separated by spaces. Tracks words from left to right. Names upper and lower case alphabet. Identifies some ending punctuation.	Demonstrates understanding of the organization and basic features of print.
Phonological Awareness	Remains silent. Does not comprehend simple spoken words. Does not distinguish syllables and individual sounds in words.	Comprehends simple words and sentences. Follows oral directions. Isolates and pronounces the initial, medial vowel, and final sounds (phonemes) in three-phoneme (consonant-vowel-consonant, or CVC) words.	Demonstrates understanding of spoken words, syllables, and sounds (phonemes).
Phonics and Word Recognition	Uses script other than English. Lacks basic one-to-one letter-sound correspondence. Scribbles or writes approximations of letters and simple words. Cannot write own name.	Produces the primary sound or many of the most frequent sounds for each vowel and consonant. Reads common, high-frequency words by sight.	Knows and applies grade-level phonics and word analysis skills in decoding words.
Fluency	Unable to decode simple words in a sentence.	Reads simple text with some accuracy, pacing, and expression. Self-corrects some errors.	Reads with sufficient accuracy and fluency to support comprehension. Self-corrects errors.

of the Foundational Skill for Reading. Performance level 2 describes developing, or approaching, grade level foundational reading skills; and performance level 1 indicates undeveloped foundational reading skills in English. These simple PLDs arrayed with CCSS Foundational Skills in Reading facilitate quick discernment and selection of appropriate strategies for instructional support. I will be referring to these levels for differentiating instruction throughout the book.

Structure of the Book

Before we can jump into the four domains of foundational reading skills, we need to address a central concept of CCSS as defined by Standard 10 Range, Quality, and Complexity. Chapter 2 of this book, "Connecting Foundational Skills, ELLs, and Standard 10," defines the concepts of range, quality, and text complexity and critiques an exclusively text-centric approach to reading as it relates to instruction for ELLs. The assumption of the framers of the Common Core is that climbing a staircase of ever increasing levels of text complexity will lead to college readiness. Teaching ELLs to read, however, requires contextual support in order to increase text complexity. Our job as teachers is not to make instruction difficult and confusing; it is to provide meaningful contexts for learning. We are called to help ELLs climb the "staircase of complexity," not descend in a spiral of confusion and frustration. This chapter makes explicit the refrain, *context supports complexity*, to help ELLs climb with comprehension and skill.

Chapter 3 provides an overview of each of the four domains of the Foundational Skills in Reading: Print Concepts, Phonological Awareness, Phonics and Word Recognition, and Fluency. Each domain is defined according the component standards provided by CCSS. In addition, I discuss how ELLs require particular instructional considerations for each domain. This chapter challenges many conventionally held ideas about beginning reading instruction. Let's give up the notion that all children learn to read the exact same way. There are multiple factors that go into learning to read. When teaching ELLs to read, if our instruction is not meaningful from the outset, we waste valuable time as teachers and our students fall behind. Providing integrated and interconnected instruction within a meaningful context is the most efficient way to benefit ELLs.

Chapter 4 begins teaching ELLs Foundational Skills in Reading by domain. The first domain is Print Concepts, which according to CCSS is taught only in Kindergarten and 1st grade. Print concepts are comprised of identifying consonants and vowels, noting word separation, and utilizing punctuation. With ELLs, there are instructional considerations for each concept about print that are examined. Additionally, the parallels between how these print concepts developed historically and how they develop in children are fun and fascinating. Both the historical roots and developmental acquisition of letters, words, and punctuation are explored and discussed. The chapter concludes with differentiated strategies and activities matched to each of the standards that are most beneficial for ELLs.

Chapter 5 explores developing Phonological Awareness with ELLs. Like Print Concepts in the previous chapter, the CCSS addresses Phonological Awareness only in kindergarten and 1st-grade standards. According to CCSS, there are four components to Phonemic Awareness: Distinguishing vowel sounds; orally blending sounds, including consonant blends; isolating and orally pronouncing initial, medial vowel, and final sounds in words; and segmenting words into a sequence of individual sounds. Contrary to conventional thinking, helpful approaches to teaching phonological awareness to ELLs includes using visual cues with pocket mirrors to see how sounds are formed in the mouth, and using touch to feel the buzz of voiced consonants and feel lip rounding for sounds like /-oo-/. Each of the corresponding standards for phonological awareness will be provided with exemplary activities for instruction of ELLs.

Chapter 6 presents Phonics and Word Recognition. The CCSS got it right when it placed these two components together. Think of how these two modalities work together, auditory and visual. Phonics is not without its strong proponents and detractors. As Moustafa (2014) reminds us, it is not a question of if we should teach phonics; it is a matter of how we teach. Shanahan (2006) argued, based on the research literature, that phonics is best taught in a context-rich way that connects learning to whole texts. The analytical, or more contextual, approach is particularly helpful for ELLs because what they learn must first be tied to meaningful literacy experiences. The same applies to word recognition, which loses meaning when taught in isolation. The distinctions between words like "read" and "read" are meaningless without context. The CCSS for Phonics and Word Recognition apply across the entire K–5 grade range. So this chapter includes instructional recommendations for each standard, K–5.

Chapter 7 defines and applies a range of strategies for fluency instruction for ELLs. Reading fluency, as defined by the National Reading Panel (2000) and Samuels (2006), means reading with accuracy, automaticity, and with prosody, or expression. The CCSS has a high degree of overlapping standards K–5, so I've grouped them for instructional purposes according to the following categories: Purpose and Understanding (K–5), Accuracy and Prosody (1–5), and Contextual Support and Self-Correction (1–5). Fluency is an area where teachers can have a lot of fun. In addition to repeated reading activities, teachers can have ELLs recite poetry, sing songs, chant, apply drama and theater, and compete to read for practice. Use of culturally relevant materials is highly encouraged to increase fluency. Additionally, quality use of appropriate digital media can have a significant impact on fluency development for ELLs.

At this point in the book, the focus shifts from specific Foundational Skills in Reading to lesson planning in alignment with CCSS. Chapter 8 addresses in detail how to write a CCSS-aligned lesson plan to teach foundational reading skills that are differentiated for ELLs. Consider the task of putting together Common Core, Foundational Skills in Reading, and differentiated instruction. Add to the mix, authentic assessment of student learning outcomes. This can be a conundrum for any teacher. Therefore, I provide a lesson template with instructions for each component of the planning process including preliminary information, instructional procedures, and assessment of outcomes. Some other features include ensuring consistent alignment with CCSS at each segment of the lesson plan, an exemplar lesson plan, and a lesson template available from the Routledge website at www.routledge.com/books/details/9781138017696.

Chapter 9 concludes the book by bringing together the entire notion of teaching ELLs to read at the foundational skills level by providing a collection of exemplary lesson plans for each grade level, K–5. The plans are designed to address CCSS performance tasks for reading informational texts. They address standards from both Foundational Skills and Informational Texts in order to illustrate how to integrate and interconnect instruction. As stated earlier, if our work is not useful and applicable to classroom settings, it is not rigorous. Therefore, each of the lesson plans are designed around performance tasks drawn from the ELA-CCSS Appendix B-Text Exemplars and Sample Performance Tasks (CCSS, 2010).

References

August, D. E., & Shanahan, T. E. (2006). *Developing literacy in second-language learners: Report of the National Literacy Panel on Language-Minority Children and Youth*. Mahwah, NJ: Lawrence Erlbaum Associates Publishers.

Boyd-Batstone, P. (2006). *Differentiated early literacy for English language learners: Practical strategies*. Boston: Allyn & Bacon.

Boyd-Batstone, P. (2013). *Helping English Language Learners meet the Common Core: Assessment and instructional Strategies K–12*. New York: Routledge.

Burkhardt, H., & Schoenfeld, A. H. (2003). Improving educational research: Toward a more useful, more influential, and better-funded enterprise. *Educational Researcher*, 32(9), 3–14.

Cummins, J. (1994). Knowledge, power, and identity in teaching English as a second language. In F. Genesee, Ed., *Educating second language children: The whole child, the whole curriculum, the whole community*, pp. 33–58. New York: Cambridge University Press.

Griffin, P., Burns, M. S., & Snow, C. E. (Eds.). (1998). *Preventing reading difficulties in young children*. Washington, DC: National Academies Press.

Moustafa, M. (2014). Improving the Common Core's Foundational Skills in Reading, K–2. *The California Reader*, 48(1), 11–19.

National Governors Association. (2010). Common core state standards. www.corestandards.org/

National Reading Panel (US), National Institute of Child Health, & Human Development (US). (2000). *Report of the national reading panel: Teaching children to read: An evidence-based assessment of the scientific research literature on reading and its implications for reading instruction: Reports of the subgroups*. National Institute of Child Health and Human Development, National Institutes of Health.

Samuels, S. J. (2006). Toward a model of reading fluency. In S. J. Samuels & A. E. Farstrup, Eds., *What research has to say about fluency instruction*, pp. 24–46. Newark, DE: International Reading Association.

Shanahan, T. (2006). The National Reading Panel Report: Practical advice for teachers. www.learningpt.org/pdfs/literacy/nationalreading.pdf

2

Connecting Foundational Skills, ELLs, and Standard 10
Range, Quality, and Complexity in Context

Following the English Language Arts (ELA) domains of the Common Core State Standards (Reading, Writing, Listening and Speaking) is Standard 10: Range, Quality, and Complexity. On the surface, Standard 10 may appear to stand apart from the other ELA standards; it also does not provide guidance to teaching ELLs to read at the foundational skills level. For example, beginning ELL readers, by definition, have a limited reading range and may not be able to comprehend complex texts in English.

Standard 10 represents a central focus that is integral to CCSS. Applying Standard 10 means establishing habits of mind at the foundational level for planning, teaching, and learning, which will address range, quality, and complexity. Standard 10 can be folded into teaching foundational reading skills; but teachers must develop the perspective of a professional educator, who makes informed decisions about appropriate instruction for ELLs.

In this chapter, the three descriptors of Standard 10, range, quality, and complexity, are defined. The overarching theme of Standard 10 of text complexity is discussed and critiqued. In addition we'll explore its application and challenges, particularly with regard to instruction for ELLs at the foundational skills level. The expectation is that range, quality, and complexity are supported and mediated by school district systems in general; but it is up to the classroom teacher, as an educational professional, to interpret and directly apply the standards to instruction for ELLs on a daily basis. The key to increasing complexity is to provide meaningful materials and instruction rich with context for ELLs. It's not just about texts; it's about context.

Defining Standard 10: Range, Quality, and Complexity for ELLs

The image that captures the central idea behind CCSS is a "staircase of complexity," illustrating children rising from initial schooling to college and career readiness (Figure 2.1).

According to the framers of the CCSS, "One of the key requirements of the Common Core State Standards for Reading is that all students must be able to comprehend texts of steadily increasing complexity as they progress through school. By the time they complete the core, students must be able to read and comprehend independently and proficiently the kinds of complex texts commonly found in college and careers" (CCSS Appendix-A, p. 1).

Standard 10 represents an overarching theme employed by CCSS to inculcate the ever-increasing complexity of texts and tasks needed to prepare students for college and careers. However, defining terms is somewhat of a challenge. The descriptive words assigned to Standard 10, "Range, Quality, and Complexity," are ambiguous and open to wide interpretation. For example in Appendix-A of the CCSS, the word "Range" is used four different ways to describe very different things. "Quality" is unspecific, and not defined in a measurable way, but it is used to stress that high standards are in place. "Complexity" is the central concept behind Standard 10 and a tri-part formula is applied to measure the complexity of texts. "Text complexity" is the only term defined in the glossary of terms in Appendix-A of the CCSS. But the measures for complexity are left open for others to select and interpret.

Figure 2.1 Staircase of Complexity

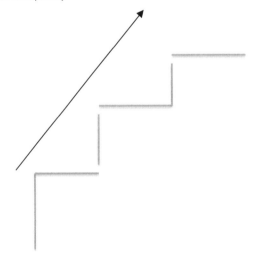

Defining Terms

Range: The word is used in the following ways with reference to Standard 10, CCSS Appendix-A:

1. The **range** of types of texts and topics, time periods, cultures, and genres.
2. Text complexity band—A **range** of text difficulty corresponding to grade spans within the Standards; specifically, the spans from grades 2–3, grades 4–5, grades 6–8, grades 9–10, and grades 11–CCR (college and career readiness).
3. The **range** of texts according to readability scores represented by Lexiles scales.
4. The **range** of scaffolding and support teachers provide for students at each grade level as they moved from decoding text to independent reading with high levels of comprehension.

Quality: The word "quality" is used in connection with "high-quality" materials such as significant literary selections; current, valid, reliable, and accurate informational texts; and current and comprehensive reference materials.

Complexity: Simply put, the framers of the CCSS call for increasing levels of complexity of reading materials to comprehend and learning tasks to complete.

According to the CCSS Glossary of Terms: "Text **complexity**—The inherent difficulty of reading and comprehending a text combined with consideration of reader and task variables; in the Standards, a three-part assessment of text difficulty that pairs qualitative and quantitative measures with reader-task considerations" (p. 43).

A Three-Part Model for Measuring Text Complexity

The following numbered components of the measures of text complexity are taken verbatim from the CCSS. Below each dimension, I've inserted my own comments as they pertain to Foundational Skills in Reading with ELLs.

1. **Qualitative Dimensions of Text Complexity.** In the Standards, qualitative dimensions and qualitative factors refer to those aspects of text complexity best measured or only measurable by an attentive human reader, such as levels of meaning or purpose, structure, language conventionality and clarity, and knowledge demands (CCSS Appendix-A, p. 4).

The qualitative dimension of text complexity allows teachers to determine the most appropriate reading materials for instruction. This places the burden of responsibility on the teacher to ensure that ELLs are reading meaningful and purposeful material. With ELLs the primary concern is meaningful reading experiences. In addition to selecting well-illustrated texts to enhance meaning, ELLs will benefit greatly from using texts and media, which represent their own culture and milieu.

Let's look at this from the ELLs perspective. Imagine that you are a newly immigrated student in a school in Helsinki, Finland. The teacher hands you a text to read in *Suomen Kieli*, the primary Finnish language. The text meets all the criteria of the qualitative dimensions of text complexity in that it is purposeful, well-structured, uses proper language conventions, is clearly written for native Finns, and provides well-researched information from reputable sources. However, until the text is made meaningful to you, it is no more than markings on a page. Even if the Finnish teacher reads the text aloud to you, it most likely would sound like incomprehensible noise, without meaning.

Therefore, the primary criterion for qualitative selection of texts is a matter of what comes first. Meaningful texts providing rich context must be the first concern of teachers of ELLs. When all the other criteria can be met with texts that provide meaningful messages to ELLs, the teacher has found a golden resource. But if the text is meaningless, all of the other criteria become moot.

2. **Quantitative Dimensions of Text Complexity.** The terms quantitative dimensions and quantitative factors refer to those aspects of text complexity, such as word length or frequency, sentence length, and text cohesion, that are difficult if not impossible for a human reader to evaluate efficiently, especially in long texts, and are thus today typically measured by computer software (CCSS Appendix-A, p. 4).

Here I am reminded of a sign that hung in Albert Einstein's office at Princeton University:

Not everything that counts can be counted, and not everything that can be counted counts. (1995)

Teachers can expect that publishers will provide the quantitative measures of text complexity as they publish and reprint reading materials. There are a number of scales to calculate readability and complexity. Keep in mind that the formulae for calculating such scores are more valid with informational texts than literary texts. The military and the medical field employ readability scales to help compose easy-to-read directions for military operations and clear information on prescribed medications. But be advised that those are limited kinds of informational texts that attempt to convey a singular type of message. Word length, sentence length, and so forth may accurately measure readability of a specific text type; but they do not determine the complexity of profound and elegant sentences used in other genres.

To explore readability scales, I submitted a paragraph from this book for analysis of text complexity to Readability-Score.com, a free website that applies six different readability scales to written texts. The site calculated one readability score and five different grade level scales and then calculated an average score to compute what grade level the text is suited for. The average grade level for the writing in this book is approximately senior year of high school, freshman year of college (12.4) level text. That score is what you would expect for a text like this one.

In contrast, I submitted a Rene Descartes's quote, "I think, therefore I am" (1637), to Readability-Score.com. The results were perplexing, at best. The Flesch-Kincaid Reading Ease Score was 83.3 (1–100 point scale—the higher the number the easier to read). The Flesch-Kincaid Grade level scale was approximately 3rd grade level (2.9); the Gunning-Fog score was 10th grade (10); the Coleman-Liau Index was 5th grade (5.3); the SMOG Index was 6th grade (6); and the Automated Readability Index was preschool (–2). In sum, the quantitative measures could not capture the depth and elegance of the sentence.

The lessons to take away from this are that we should take quantitative measures with a grain of skepticism. Note that elegance and profundity are not measurable using quantitative tools "not everything that counts can be counted . . ." Further, anytime we rely on quantitative measures of text, we should compare the results to what we know is appropriate and meaningful for ELLs to read ". . . and not everything that can be counted counts."

3. **Reader and Task Considerations.** While the prior two elements of the model focus on the inherent complexity of text, variables specific to particular readers (such as motivation, knowledge, and experiences) and to particular tasks (such as purpose and the complexity of the task assigned and the questions posed) must also be considered when determining whether a text is appropriate for a given student. Such assessments are best made by teachers employing their professional judgment, experience, and knowledge of their students and the subject (CCSS Appendix-A, p. 4).

The reader and the task are the teacher's primary considerations. There are a number of ways that all students can experience written text and develop habits of mind called for by CCSS. Note how the framers of the CCSS identify one way to foster reading experiences in the early grades with reference to Standard 10:

> children in the early grades (particularly K–2) should participate in rich, structured conversations with an adult in response to the written texts that are read aloud, *orally* comparing and contrasting as well as analyzing and synthesizing, in the manner called for by the Standards. (CCSS Standard 10)

Teachers of ELLs need to concentrate on the third component of text-complexity "Reader and task considerations." When the reader is an ELL, just because their English is limited, does not mean that they cannot think profoundly about a subject. To refer back to an earlier example, just because I can't read in *Suomen Kieli*, the primary Finnish language, doesn't mean that I can't think and comprehend deep and complex ideas. Too often ELLs are given cognitively undemanding tasks because teachers make the false assumption that they lack intelligence due to their limited English skills. Let's not make those kinds of false assumptions about our students.

Standard 10 Assumptions and Foundational Skills for ELLs: Text Complexity Is a Direction, not a Destination

The Common Core expectation, or goal, is college and career readiness. I would add that the goal of reading instruction is that students will eventually become skilled, independent readers, who share in the joy of the reading experience. The Common Core standards are a set of expectations based on a combination of research and assumption. The concern here is the reliance on untested assumptions for such a large-scale project as CCSS. The assumptions, center on the following: trajectory, expectations for struggling readers—who are oftentimes ELLs, and text complexity ubiquitously applied. These concerns are intensified as we try to connect Standard 10 to Foundational Skills in Reading.

Pearson and Hiebert (2013) and Hiebert (2012) pointed out two assumptions from the writers of the CCSS, which have little if any basis in the research with regard to early readers grade 2 and above. Those assumptions pertain to trajectory and expectations for struggling readers. There is no research evidence to support the assumption that a 2nd grade reader will do better in college if provided with complex texts. She goes on to consider the question, what is the optimal trajectory for young readers? The concern is not whether students should push their boundaries and stretch their reading palette; but at what point. What is optimal text complexity for early readers?

Pearson and Hiebert (2013) also considered the assumption of unrealistic expectations for struggling readers. In other words, if we continue to supply texts that were already inaccessible to children, do we simply tell them to just try harder? Here the question addresses what activities and supports do young readers need. This is particularly apropos to the target population of this book, English language learners, who struggle to learn a new language as they learn to read. Text complexity is not the sole, primary concern with ELLs. Providing meaningful, engaging, and culturally relevant texts that may address complexity is ideal; but not as a first priority. The first concern with ELLs is reading for meaning, more on this throughout the book.

Shanahan (2013) spoke to the fundamental shift in the CCSS from an activities-centric approach to a text-centric approach. The CCSS staircase assumption is that supplying ever increasingly difficult texts will produce more sophisticated readers. The concern is that "children may be asked to read texts that we once would have claimed to be at a frustration level" (p. 189). He did point out that the writers of the CCSS intentionally did not set text levels for grades K and 1. I would, however, add that consistently insisting that children read at a frustration level would be a mindless application of text complexity and might lead to opposite expectations, namely children becoming unmotivated and losing the joy of reading due to consistently reading at a frustration level.

A staircase is not a destination; it is one pathway. Increasing text complexity is not a goal; it is a direction. Developing skilled, independent readers who share in the joy of rich reading experiences is a goal. If teachers and administrators use the notion of text complexity as a direction, they become the professionals who make important instructional decisions with regard to text complexity to meet the ultimate goal of their teaching. Teachers are informed practitioners, who decide pacing, apply appropriate strategies, and consult about materials selection. They can be skeptical and call for evidence to apply a particular approach. Recognizing that there is a significant dose of untested assumptions built into the CCSS, we need to be thoughtful practitioners, who have honed a professional's perspective of our students' needs and appropriate instructional applications.

In the next section, we will explore this notion further in reference to a model developed by Cummins (1986/2001), which provides a framework for addressing cognitively demanding material and tasks in meaningful ways.

Helping ELLs Climb the Staircase of Complexity Instead of Descending the Spiral of Confusion

I've argued that what helps ELLs climb the staircase of complexity is to, first of all, provide meaningful tasks and materials. Without understanding what they hear, read, and do, instead of climbing the staircase of complexity, ELLs will descend a spiral of confusion and frustration. Our job is **not** to make Foundational Skills difficult and confusing. Until we provide what is meaningful to ELLs, we cannot successfully move along a continuum of complexity. The key is context, context, and more context.

In this section, I discuss a cognitive model to help us think about how to help ELLs climb the staircase of complexity. Then I will show how a CCSS literacy task can be adapted to address foundational domains in reading in a context-rich format.

I've found the work of Cummins (1986/2001) very helpful in understanding context-embedded instruction. He conceived of a cognitive model that gives us the key to addressing Standard 10, and text complexity (see Figure 2.2) with ELLs. The model represents two interesting continuum about instructional tasks and materials for ELLs. The North/South, or y-axis, is a continuum of cognitively undemanding (read "simplistic") to cognitively demanding (read "complex") tasks and materials. The West/East, or x-axis, continuum represents context-embedded (read "rich with meaning") to context-reduced (read "dense") tasks and materials.

Cognitively demanding tasks and materials (Table 2.1) include a complex project utilizing challenging texts, problem solving, teamwork, multiple steps, and the production of a final product to present to others—the type of task that Standard 10 calls for.

Cognitively undemanding tasks (Table 2.2) and materials are useful, simple, easy on the brain, and limited. They may include listening to a simple

Figure 2.2 Jim Cummins's Cognitive Model

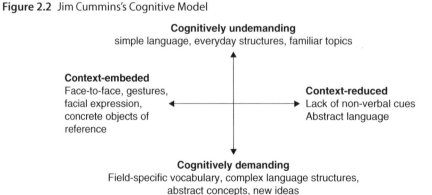

Table 2.1 Cognitively Demanding Tasks and Materials

Cognitively demanding	
Tasks	**Materials**
• Learning a language	• Research articles
• Learning to play a musical instrument	• Novels
• Problem solving approaches	• Poetry
• Teamwork and collaboration	• Textbooks
• Justifying one's conclusions	• Content specific terminology
• Process writing (envisioning, drafting, editing, revising, publishing)	• Sheet music
• Constructing a persuasive argument	• Computer hardware/software
• Creative use of media and digital tools	• Video equipment
• Multi-step projects	• Internet sites and search tools
• Developing creative products	• Primary source documents
• Dramatic productions	• Archival footage of historical events
• Public presentations of completed work	• Artifacts from other periods and cultures

Table 2.2 Cognitively Undemanding Tasks and Materials

Cognitively undemanding	
Tasks	**Materials**
• Listening to a well-read story	• Picture books with few words
• Reciting a short/simple poem	• Predictable books
• Reading short/simple texts	• Coloring books
• Singing familiar songs	• Some comic books
• Cut and paste projects	• Illustrated worksheets
• Viewing simple movies	• Some simple videos
• Single-step projects	• Precut and paste clip art
• Selecting multiple choice answers	
• Providing one-word replies	

story, reciting easy poems, singing familiar songs, viewing videos about simple topics, and cutting out pictures to paste next to words.

Context-embedded tasks and materials (Table 2.3) include vivid illustrations, cultural relevance, familiar activities, primary language support, social interaction, and quality and timely feedback.

Context-reduced tasks and materials (Table 2.4) include students working silently at their individual desks deciphering dense texts without context clues such as illustrations, well-defined vocabulary, media support, or primary language support.

In order to address Standard 10, teachers want to develop students who successfully engage with cognitively demanding tasks and materials, and who can comprehend context-reduced material. Looking back to the Cummins (1986/2001) model, ELLs begin learning in cognitively undemanding settings that are richly context-embedded; but they move to more cognitively demanding tasks and material through context-embedded instruction. Once they have gained knowledge and skills via highly context-embedded instruction, they are then prepared to address cognitively demanding tasks and materials in context-reduced settings.

Table 2.3 Context-embedded Tasks and Materials

Context-embedded	
Tasks	**Materials**
• Project-based learning	• Handling real objects
• Socially interactive (pairs and teams)	• Vividly illustrated
• Self-selected options (choice)	• Field trips
• Personally meaningful (interactive-journaling, letter writing, blogging)	• Multi-media
• Highly engaging (public products)	• Culturally relevant
• Inviting creativity (poetry, song, artwork; building and constructing)	• Current events
• Results in a change in the classroom, school, or community (socially responsible)	• Locally situated
• Quality feedback (authentic assessment from peers and teacher)	• Rich, descriptive language with well-defined terminology
	• Supported by the primary language

Table 2.4 Context-reduced Tasks and Materials

Context-reduced	
Tasks	**Materials**
• Individualized assignments	• Dense texts without illustrations
• Silent reading without knowing the background and/or cultural context of the text	• Reference texts
• Copying definitions from a glossary	• Abstract formulae
• Outlining subject matter from a textbook	• Data tables
• Summarizing a text	• Research articles
• Homework problems at the back of the book	• Materials from another time period or culture without orientation
• Deciphering directions without illustrations	• Dictionary definitions
• Standardized tests and scores	• Texts only in English
• Summative evaluation results	

Foundational Skills Activities

To show what I mean, I'll apply context-embedded instruction to Foundational Skills in order to prepare students to do a CCSS performance task. To apply the task first, without providing context rich tasks and materials, would risk confusion and frustration. Instead, the students are asked to work through each of the areas of Foundational Skills in order to be ready to address the CCSS performance task.

Below, I've adapted one of the suggested performance tasks from CCSS Appendix-B (p. 53). I selected a poem by Gary Soto (1999/1995) because he uses English and Spanish idiomatic expressions in such rich and diverse ways. Teachers can use the poetry to provide context. He also uses images that are common to the experience of many Latino children, thus providing a more culturally relevant text.

> **CCSS Performance Task:** Students read Gary Soto's poem "Eating while Reading," determining the meaning of words and phrases in the poem, particularly focusing on identifying his use of non-literal language in reference to reading and eating (e.g., "this sweet dance")

and talking about how it suggests meaning (Adapted from CCSS Appendix-B, p. 53).

Context-rich Materials: Collect each of the items mentioned in the poem (book, bubble gum, sunflower seeds, soda, beef jerky). Search for Internet pictures of some of the following: taffy being turned in a vat, red snow cone dripping down the arms of a child, and a sticky red face dripping with sweets. Additional materials: Copies of the poem, scissors, glue, paper, and pencils.

Print Concepts: Objects and Pictures to Words: Read the poem several times to the class. As the teacher reads the first time, show each object mentioned in the poem and identify the corresponding word (book, bubble gum, sunflower seeds, soda, beef jerky) and displays the pictures referenced in the poem (taffy being turned in a vat, red snow cone dripping down the arms of a child, and a sticky red face dripping with sweets). Ask the students to point to the item and the corresponding word as it is read the second time. (Alternate activities: Find the two questions in the poem. How do questions begin? How do questions end? Also, match the phrases that begin with "Or" to the objects on display.)

Phonological Awareness: What is the difference between -oo- and **-oo-**? Show the words BOOK and BALL**OO**N to the group with corresponding pictures. Write the words on a dry-erase board, but highlight the **-oo-** in red in each word. Point out that even though they both have **-oo-**, they sound different. Ask students to place their hand lightly on their throats as they say the word "book"—note the buzzing and the short -uh- sound. Then ask them to place their hands on their lips as they slowly say "ball**ooooo**n." Note how the lips purse outward to say **-ooooo-**. Then ask the students to get another book of their choice and search for words that have -oo-. When they find an -oo- word, they must decide which group the -oo- sound goes with. Then list the words below BO**O**K, for the short -uh- sound, or BALL**OO**N, for the lip-rounded **-ooooo-** sound.

Phonics and Word Recognition: Double-consonant and Consonant-blend word search: Give each student a copy of the poem. Group them in pairs, or in threes, depending if you have an even or odd number of students. Give each pair or trio a copy of the poem. Before you get started show examples of double-consonants in words (lit-tle, fi**dd**le, se**ss**ion); and consonant-blends (**fl**ower, **bl**ue, **st**ill). Tell them that they have 5 minutes to create two lists of word families: one list of double-consonant words, and another list of words with consonant-blends. Find as many words as you can. Compare lists for accuracy. Discuss the meaning of each word.

Fluency: Group poem recitation: Cut up the poem into stanzas, example: "What is better/Than this book/And the churn of candy/In your mouth." Give each student in a small group of students a short stanza or two to memorize. After five minutes of memorizing the stanza, have the students line up in the order of the poem. Ask the group to recite the poem for the class. With smaller groups the students will need to change the line up as they take turns reciting the stanzas in order. This task can be made more complex by increasing the amount of text to be recited.

Performance Task for Increased Complexity: Now that the poem has been pulled apart and analyzed according to Foundational Skills, the students can discuss the poem in terms of the non-literal meaning of phrases like "this sweet dance." Students can identify other non-literal phrases in the poem, and even compose their own lines that exhibit non-literal phrases.

This is analogous to learning to play piano and to read music. This past year, my wife gave me the present of a year's worth of piano lessons. I'd never played piano before. I had excellent instruction and worked on simple musical texts. The goal was to become a skilled musician; but it takes time. As I slowly developed a modicum of skill, I was supported by activities to increase my strength and dexterity, given help to recognize notes and then chords at a glance, I repeatedly played simple melodies to increase my fluency and fluidity. I wasn't just provided increasingly difficult musical texts. I was given a range of meaningful support to help me move to more complex tasks and material. The following chapter outlines how each of the Foundational Skills in Reading may be taught with special consideration of the unique needs of ELLs.

References

Common Core State Standards. Appendix-A & B. www.corestandards.org/assets/Appendix_A.pdf

Cummins, J. (2001). Empowering minority students: A framework for intervention. *Harvard Educational Review Classic reprint. Harvard Educational*

Review, 71(4), 656–675 (reprint of 1986 article in *Harvard Educational Review*).

Descartes, R. (1637). Quote in part IV of his work, *Discourse on Method of Rightly Conducting One's Reason and of Seeking the Truth in the Sciences*. Project Gutenberg: www.gutenberg.org/ebooks/59

Einstein, A. Copyright: Kevin Harris 1995 (may be freely distributed with this acknowledgement). http://rescomp.stanford.edu/~cheshire/EinsteinQuotes.html

Hiebert, E.H. (2012). The Common Core's staircase of complexity: Getting the size of the first step right. *Reading Today*, 29(3), 26–27.

Pearson, P.D. & Hiebert, E.H. (2013). Understanding the Common Core State Standards. In Lesley Morrow, Tim Shanahan, & Karen Wixson, Eds., *Teaching with the Common Core Standards for English language arts: PreK–2*, pp. 1–21. New York: Guilford Press.

Shanahan, T. (2013). On implementing the Common Core Standards successfully, Grades K–2. In Leslie Mandell Morrow, Timothy Shanahan, Karen Wixson, Eds. *Teaching with the English Language Common Core Standards for English Language Arts, K–2*. New York: Guilford Press.

Soto, G. (1999/1995). Eating while reading. In *The 20th Century Children's Poetry Treasury* (selected by Jack Prelutsky). New York: Knopf.

3

Common Core Foundational Skills in Reading and ELLs

What Are Foundational Skills in Reading?

The writers of the Common Core State Standards (CCSS) identified four domains of foundational reading skills that were drawn from the previous work of the National Reading Panel (NRP, 2000). The purpose of this chapter is to define each domain of the foundational reading skills and to point out the unique considerations ELLs pose for instruction in each area. The four domains are as follows:

1. **Print Concepts**: understanding the organization and basic features of print
2. **Phonological Awareness**: understanding spoken words, syllables, and sounds (phonemes)
3. **Phonics and Word Recognition**: knowing and applying grade-level phonics and word analysis skills in decoding words
4. **Fluency**: reading emergent-reader texts with purpose and understanding

Differentiating Foundational Skills for English Learners

A significant contribution of CCSS is the establishment of foundational reading skills as a starting place rather than an end goal of reading. Whereas the

National Reading Panel (NRP, 2000) limited its scope of the reading process to the above four domains, plus comprehension and vocabulary, the CCSS has taken a much broader view of reading. The goal for the teacher with foundational reading skills is to equip all students with an "understanding and working knowledge of concepts of print, the alphabetic principle, and other basic conventions of the English writing system" (CCSS, 2010).

The four foundational skills are designated for grades K–5, while comprehension and vocabulary are expanded and developed across all grade levels. Rightly so, foundational reading skills are limited to elementary grade levels; but ELLs pose special considerations with regard to foundational reading skills. There are factors beyond grade level to consider. One important factor is native language proficiency, also called primary language (L_1) literacy, which has a dramatic impact on foundational reading skills in English. English language learners will arrive in the classroom with a wide range of L_1 and English literacy development.

The writers of the CCSS called for a differentiated approach to reading instruction when they stated that "instruction should be differentiated: good readers will need much less practice with these concepts than struggling readers will. The point is to teach students what they need to learn and not what they already know—to discern when particular children or activities warrant more or less attention" (CCSS, 2010). Differentiation has rarely been applied to foundational literacy to any significant degree. Formative assessment tools help the teacher discern reading skill levels, but an understanding of the L_1 literacy of ELLs is essential to differentiate instruction appropriately.

Language instruction and reading instruction have different starting points. Conventional reading instruction has had the tendency to approach foundational skills as the only starting point for all learners. In fact, when teachers recognize language differences and understand that each ELL brings strengths and needs to foundational literacy, they begin to differentiate instruction in beneficial ways. For instance, students who speak a tonal language have a much greater acuity for sound–symbol relationships than native English speakers, for example. Some ELLs will be quite literate in their home language, while others may not read or write in their own language. Having some insight into the ELLs' primary language proficiency will establish how to differentiate foundational skills in reading. I hope that we keep this point in mind as we work to differentiate instruction for English language learners.

To further illustrate the need to differentiate foundational skills in reading for ELLs, Torlakson (2012) outlined three categories of English language learners according to their L_1 literacy:

1. No, or little, L_1 print literacy; in some cases, the primary language is unwritten (e.g., Hmong Daw)

2. Foundational L₁ literacy in non-alphabetic and/or not Latin-based languages (e.g., Arabic, Hindi, Chinese, Korean)
3. Foundational L₁ literacy in Latin-based alphabetic languages (e.g., Spanish)

Some ELLs readily develop into good readers; others need considerable scaffolding to establish foundational skills.

Print Concepts: Understanding the Organization and Basic Features of Print

These standards are directed toward fostering students' understanding and working knowledge of concepts of print, the alphabetic principle, and other basic conventions of the English writing system. (CCSS ELA Reading Foundational Skills: Introduction, 2010)

Print Concepts, according to Common Core State Standards, are defined by five attributes:

1. Understanding the organization and basic features of print.
2. Following words from left to right, top to bottom, and page-by-page.
3. Recognizing spoken words as represented in written language by specific sequences of letters.
4. Seeing words as separated by spaces in print.
5. Recognizing and naming all upper- and lowercase letters of the alphabet.

Let's look at each one of these attributes of Print Concepts. First of all, "understanding the organization and basic features of print" is an umbrella statement for the following four attributes of Print Concepts. Items 2 and 3 refer to organization of print; and items 4 and 5 refer to features of print. The second attribute, "following words from left to right, top to bottom, and page-by-page" describes how print is organized on a page. Xu (2014) pointed out that Chinese, in particular Mandarin-speaking English learners, have particular challenges with print literacy in English. One of those challenges is recognizing a different orientation of print on the page. The next organizational attribute of print is "recognizing spoken words as represented in written language by specific sequences of letters." For English learners, a benchmark shift in literacy is when they begin to move from solely oral communication to using print as a means to communicate. Moving ELLs from oral to print communication begins when they recognize print as significant and how sequences of letters are arranged in meaningful ways.

The last two attributes of Print Concepts focus on features of print itself. The feature of identifying separate words as opposed to strings of letters, or "seeing words as separated by spaces in print." Interestingly, ELLs may already have this skill in place prior to learning English because this is a feature of a vast number of written languages. The final feature of print in English is that it is alphabetic, "recognizing and naming all upper- and lowercase letters of the alphabet." Again Xu (2014) reminds us that not all languages are alphabetic; therefore ELLs may require additional instruction to recognize and name all upper- and lowercase letters, which will be discussed further in Chapter 4.

Phonological Awareness: Understanding Spoken Words, Syllables, and Sounds (Phonemes)

> These foundational skills are not an end in and of themselves; rather, they are necessary and important components of an effective, comprehensive reading program designed to develop proficient readers with the capacity to comprehend texts across a range of types and disciplines. (CCSS ELA Reading Foundational Skills: Introduction, 2010)

Phonology and phonics tend to mistakenly be used interchangeably; however, they represent a different set of foundational skills. Phonology draws its roots from the field of Linguistics in language instruction (Ladefoged, 1995); whereas phonics has commercial and popular roots in reading instruction. In fact, until an ELL has a strong grasp of phonemes in English, phonics instruction will be a meaningless activity. Phonemes as defined by the Oxford Dictionary (n.d.) is "Any of the perceptually distinct units of sound in a specified language that distinguish one word from another, for example p, b, d, and t in the English words pad, pat, bad, and bat."

Note the phrase "perceptually distinct units of sound." The phrase refers to the recognition of meaningful sounds in words, or being aware of letters that make a meaningful difference in a word. It also implies the act of segmenting words into meaningful sounds. Recently I was talking with an Arabic speaking ELL from Saudi Arabia. I asked her, "When did you arrive?" and she replied, "In Monterrey Park." I had asked "When," she had heard "Where." She heard a different phoneme than the one I expressed with "whe-n." To further illustrate, in another instance, some years ago I was in Paris, France at the post office purchasing stamps for my postcards. When the clerk told me how much to pay, I heard the first part of the word, *quat-*; but I wasn't sure if I had heard *quatre* (four), *quatroze* (fourteen), or *quarante* (forty). I didn't know how much money to give the clerk, so I just put a pile of bills on the counter and let her take the amount—I hoped she was honest. I didn't have the phonemic awareness to fully distinguish meaningful units of sound, though I knew the number was related to the root word for "four."

Interestingly, Phonemic Awareness, in the Common Core parlance, is dealt with entirely on an oral language basis. In linguistics phonemes are generally presented in conjunction with their written counterparts, graphemes. However in CCSS, graphemes are addressed in the Phonics and Word Recognition standards.

According to CCSS, **Phonemic Awareness** is expressed as understanding spoken words, syllables, and sounds. It encompasses oral language, not written language. Phonemic Awareness is addressed only in kindergarten and 1st grade standards. Specifically, Phonemic Awareness in CCSS is limited to the following four elements:

1. Distinguishing vowel sounds.
2. Orally blending sounds, including consonant blends.
3. Isolating and orally pronouncing initial, medial vowel, and final sounds in words.
4. Segmenting words into a sequence of individual sounds.

For the English language learner, some sounds in English are very difficult to hear and articulate. It may seem counterintuitive, but helping the ELL see and feel how sounds are formed can be much more beneficial than asking students to attempt to repeat sounds orally. For example, seeing a vowel chart that shows where vowel sounds in the English language are formed in the mouth dramatically increases phonemic awareness. Although there are as many as 19 vowel sounds in English, note how vowels can be charted relative to their position in the mouth with a trapezoidal vowel chart. After seeing how the teacher forms specific blends in the mouth, including how to position the tongue and lips, the ELL can look at their own formation of blends looking at their mouths in the mirror. (We will discuss this further in Chapter 5.)

Phonics and Word Recognition: Knowing and Applying Grade-level Phonics and Word Analysis Skills in Decoding Words

Instruction should be differentiated: good readers will need much less practice with these concepts than struggling readers will. (CCSS ELA Reading Foundational Skills: Introduction, 2010)

Phonics is a popular notion of sound-symbol analysis. Some commercial programs identify rules for phonics instruction; others identify patterns in particular letter-sound relationships in word groups. In the National Reading Panel Report (2000), it was noted that phonics should be addressed because it had worked its way into popular notions, and commercially successful ways, of how to teach reading. There are those who claim that reading cannot be taught without extensive phonics instruction; yet profoundly deaf students continually learn to read without applying phonics. For English language learners, attention to meaningful contexts is key with phonics instruction. Without meaningful contexts, phonics instruction is reduced to parroting sounds. With CCSS, pairing phonics to word recognition and analysis is a more meaningful approach to instruction.

Shanahan (2006) pointed out that phonics instruction is generally addressed in two different ways, synthetic phonics or analytic phonics. Commercially developed products use a synthetic approach. They claim to apply a "systematic" set of rules to pronouncing letter combinations. The instruction involves examining selected rules for sound-symbol correspondences for a few minutes each day. One example rule would be applying hard c/k/ sounds when c is followed by the vowels a, o, or u, as in cat, cone, cut. Synthetic approaches are criticized for teaching phonics in isolation with rules that often have more exceptions than applications.

In contrast analytic phonics identifies sound-symbol correspondence in the context of reading a text, and uses a teaching moment to analyze the word(s) that use a particular sound-symbol correspondence. In other words, analytic phonics is paired with word recognition and analysis as recommended by the CCSS. Using word recognition and analysis as the approach to examine sound-symbol relationships provides greater meaningful contexts for instruction, thus helping ELLs learn foundational skills.

According to the CCSS, **Phonics and Word Recognition**, across kindergarten through grade 5, can be distilled to the following five foundational tasks in reading:

1. Knowing the spelling-sound correspondences of vowel teams and consonant blends.
2. Identifying and knowing the meaning of the most common prefixes and derivational suffixes.
3. Decoding words with common Latin suffixes.
4. Decoding multi-syllable words.
5. Reading grade-appropriate irregularly spelled words.

The above tasks for phonics and word recognition, in contrast to the oral language emphasis of phonemic awareness, focuses on moving a student from oral to print literacy. These tasks can be addressed analytically, during the course of reading instruction. Teachers need to provide time in their instruction each day to analyze the structure and sound in specific words that are part of their regular reading. Some helpful ways to address phonics and word analysis for ELLs have been suggested by Xu (2010), including providing examples of words from environmental print, analyzing students' names, utilizing text in media, word sorting and categorizing, and comparing word families, which will be discussed further in Chapter 6.

Fluency: Reading Emergent-Reader Texts With Purpose and Understanding

> The point is to teach students what they need to learn and not what they already know—to discern when particular children or activities warrant more or less attention. (CCSS ELA Reading Foundational Skills: Introduction, 2010)

Fluency, as defined by the National Reading Panel (2000) and Samuels (2006), is comprised of three components: accuracy, automaticity, and prosody.

◆ **Accuracy:** decoding by correctly generating phonological representations of each word, either because it is part of the reader's sight-word vocabulary or by use of a more effortful decoding strategy such as sounding out the word.

◆ **Automaticity:** quickly recognizing words with little cognitive effort or attention.

◆ **Prosody:** reading with proper phrasing and expression.

With English language learners in particular, it is essential to realize that these three components, although related to fluency, are not developmentally sequential. Prosody can be addressed before the ELL exhibits strong accuracy. For example, it is not uncommon for an ELL to exhibit a high degree of prosody, reading with proper phrasing and expression, after rehearsing lines from a play; yet at the same time reading with a low degree of accuracy in terms of phonological representations. There is also a linguistic factor at play here. There are phonological features of English that may not appear in the ELLs native language. One such example is the *schwa*, the /-uh-/ sound, which is ubiquitous in multi-syllabic words in English, but does not appear in other languages, such as Spanish. Therefore, the ELL may read with expression, but mispronounce words with the schwa embedded. Another linguistic example is inaccurately representing word endings, such as the ending sound /-t-/ for the word "laughed," that does not occur in other languages. These phonological structures may cause an ELL to mispronounce a word while reading with proper phrasing and expression.

There are essentially three aspects to **Reading Fluency** according to the CCSS:

1. Reading for purpose and understanding.
2. Reading orally with accuracy, appropriate rate, and expression.
3. Using context to confirm or self-correct word recognition and understanding, rereading as necessary.

The good news here is that reading instruction is not restricted to reading for accuracy alone. Accuracy will continually be developing with ELLs, but instruction for automaticity and prosody can be developed while full accuracy is achieved. This brings in so many enjoyable aspects of reading from the outset. Prosody and automaticity can be readily achieved in small increments with reading practice, recitation of poetry, singing songs, and the use of dramatic readings (more about this in Chapter 4).

What's Next?

The following four chapters of the book each explore a domain of Foundational Skills in Reading in depth and provide appropriate activities for ELLs according to performance level. (Chapter 4, Print Concepts; Chapter 5, Phonological Awareness; Chapter 6, Phonics and Word Recognition; and Chapter 7, Fluency.)

References

Common Core State Standards (2010). Retrieved from www.corestandards.org/ELA-Literacy/RF/introduction

Ladefoged, P. (1995). *Elements of Acoustic Phonetics*. Chicago: University of Chicago.

National Reading Panel Report (2000). Teaching children to read: An evidence-based assessment of scientific research literature on reading and its implications on reading instruction. Retrieved from www.nichd.nih.gov/publications/pubs/nrp/documents/report.pdf,www.nichd.nih.gov/publications/pubs/nrp/Pages/findings.aspx

Oxford Dictionaries.com (n.d.). Retrieved from: www.oxforddictionaries.com/us/definition/american_english/phoneme

Samuels, S.J. (2006). Toward a model of reading fluency. In S.J. Samuels & A.E. Farstrup (Eds.), *What research has to say about fluency instruction*, pp. 24–46. Newark, DE: International Reading Association.

Shanahan, T. (2006). *The National Reading Panel report: Practical advice for teachers*. Retrieved from www.learningpt.org/pdfs/literacy/nationalreading.pdf

Torlakson, T. (October 19, 2012). California State Superintendent of Education Report. Appendix B. Retrieved from www.cde.ca.gov/sp/el/er/documents/sbeapdaliteracy.pdf#search=Foundational%20skills&view=FitH&pagemode=none

Xu, H.S. (2010). *Teaching English language learners: Literacy strategies and resources for K–6*. New York: Gilford Press.

Xu, H.S. (2014). Addressing linguistic differences in literacy instruction for Chinese Mandarin speaking English learners. *The California Reader*, 47(3), 9–17.

4

Print Concepts
Kindergarten–Grade 1

Common Core Foundational Skills Standards for Print Concepts, K–1

Print Concepts, according to Common Core State Standards, are defined by six attributes:

1. Understanding the organization and basic features of print.
2. Following words from left to right, top to bottom, and page-by-page.
3. Recognizing spoken words as represented in written language by specific sequences of letters.
4. Seeing words as separated by spaces in print.
5. Recognizing and naming all upper- and lowercase letters of the alphabet.
6. Recognize the distinguishing features of a sentence (e.g., first word, capitalization, ending punctuation).

Developing Print Concepts With English Language Learners

[Print] . . . has been the tool of learning, the preserver of knowledge, and the medium of literature. Until the electronic age, it was *the* great means of communication over distances in space. (Chappell & Bringhurst 1970/1990)

Print concepts develop at a concrete level when students have meaningful experiences with books, print media, and environmental print; at a symbolic level when students match letters and words to images from their own surroundings; and at the abstract level as students draw meaning from a written text. Interestingly, the historical development of print and the individual development of print concepts have some unique parallels. There is a continuum of print development from the concrete identifier of a footprint or thumbprint to a symbolic representation of a pictograph or hieroglyph to the abstract invention of consonants and vowels. As teachers of foundational skills, we keep in mind that letters and words in English are an abstraction of things, experiences, and ideas. Teachers of English language learners especially must work to teach print concepts in ways that tap concrete experiences and utilize visual imagery to keep our instruction purposeful and meaningful.

Pictographs to Consonants and Vowels

Consonants initially were crafted as symbols of concrete objects; for example, in Semitic languages consonants carried symbolic meaning while vowels were represented in lesser ways by diacritical marks. According to John Healy (1970/1990), in his book *The History of the Alphabet*, the letter "b" came from a box-shaped pictograph, which symbolized a house because the word for house was *bét* (p. 57). As the letter moved from language to language, from Egyptian pictograph to Arabian script to Latin print, it changed in shape and shed its visual representation to become a sonic representation—a "con-sonant." The letter we recognize in English as "b" has shed the image of a house, and now abstractly represents a sound we make when we place both lips together and vocalize a buzz of air /b/.

The notion of consonants carrying stronger meaning over vowels is still evident. Look at the following words below. In the first iteration, the vowels have been removed. In the second iteration, the consonants have been removed. You can still decipher the meaning of the words without the vowels, but not when the consonants are taken away and the vowels, left standing alone, are meaningless:

C_PT_ _N	(CAPTAIN)	_A_ _AI_
D_ _BL_	(DOUBLE)	_ OU _ _ E
J _ MP	(JUMP)	_ U _ _

Coincidentally, in early literacy development of print concepts, young children begin by representing meaningful words with a string of consonants such as SNWMN (snowman), WTRMLN (watermelon), or PSCL (popsicle).

The consonants seem to be recognized first in the process as print concepts emerge.

What can be drawn from the above discussion is that print concepts develop in meaningful contexts. Our letters in English have shed their original symbolic meaning as they moved from pictographs to consonants. I am not suggesting that we teach historical changes to young children to make letters meaningful; I am suggesting, however, that we use print from the students' environment to initially show print as meaningful. Collecting and displaying and reading print as it appears to students on a regular, daily basis is a starting point. Using labels, signs, and meaningful images from the students' environment gives context to print contexts. Reading aloud quality books with vivid illustrations and providing guided reading to children also provides meaningful context to print.

Strings of Letters to Word Separation

Another historical development of print that parallels the development of individual print concepts is the shift from strings of letters to word separation, meaningful clusters of letters with spaces in between. Ancient texts did not exhibit word separation; it was a much later development. Saenger (1997) described the historical development of word separation as an evolutionary-like process in reading from reading aloud for liturgical purposes and proclamation to reading silently in order to gain knowledge and understanding.

In ancient times, only elite individuals, such as priests and scribes, were readers by profession. For centuries common people were not permitted to read; reading was only for professionals. Reading was done aloud, or in low-voiced meditative recitation, for liturgical purposes. Reading was also conducted for civic purposes as town criers read magisterial edicts and proclamations. The function of reading changed with the invention of separating strings of letters into meaningful clusters to form separate words. Word separation did not appear until the seventh and eighth centuries in places like Ireland, where scribes recorded philosophical and classical scientific texts. The shift represented a functional change from reading aloud professionally to reading silently in order to gain knowledge about the world. In essence, word separation portended the spread of knowledge sharing via the printed text.

In parallel development, children's earliest experiences with print include drawing pictures, making meaningful scribbles, and writing random strings of letters together. Gentry (2010) identified how moving from strings of letters to word separation is a significant development in print concepts via developmental stages of spelling. As learners progress, they form approximations of words that still appear as strings of letters; then they form separate words, although they may be spelled in idiosyncratic ways.

This is a natural progression that all children exhibit. ELLs go through the same phases, but oftentimes they are playing catch up to the native English speakers. Insightful teachers recognize the natural progression and foster the print development with encouragement to continue to recognize and write according to one's stage of development. Heavy emphasis on grammatical and spelling correctness should be discouraged at foundational levels because it may only lead to frustration on the part of the ELL. Extensive experiences with print should be encouraged, such as appropriately modeling print, fostering manipulation of letters and experimentation with writing, and using multiple senses of sight, touch, and sound help develop print concepts.

Three Foundational Functions of Punctuation: Pauses, Breaks, and Inflection

The following discussion is intended to be illustrative rather than a comprehensive discussion of punctuation. At the foundational level, there are basically three functions of punctuation. They are pauses, breaks, and inflection. Being able to communicate the functions of pauses, breaks, and inflection can give the ELL an easy guide to recognizing and using basic punctuation accurately. Historically, punctuation developed over the centuries as oral speech was transferred to written texts. Grammarians invented marks to indicate pauses, breaks, and inflection.

Punctuation marks were intended to give the reader a chance to breathe, to pause and take a breath. In written text, some pauses are longer than others so different marks were designed to indicate a longer, or stronger, pause in the text. Note the words of the early grammarian, Ben "two pricks" Jonson, writing in the 1640s (Jonson & Gifford, 1903):

> There resteth one general affection of the whole, dispersed thorough every member thereof, as the blood is thorough the body: and consisteth in the breathing, when we pronounce any sentence. For, whereas our breath is by nature so short, that we cannot continue without a stay to speak long together; it was thought necessary as well for the speaker's ease, as for the plainer deliverance of the things, spoken to invent this means, whereby men pausing a pretty while, the whole speech might never the worse be understood. (p. 456)

Ben "two pricks" Jonson earned his nickname when he discussed the invention of a comma (,) to show a short pause between phrases, or what he called "an imperfect sentence." He described what we now call a semi-colon as "two pricks" (;) to join two sentences together. He described a period as a "full prick" (.) to mark a break, at the end of a complete, or "perfect" sentence. His use of the word pricks, think "pin pricks," referred to actual holes pricked into the paper. Paragraph indentations indicate the separation of ideas as a stronger break. In short, punctuation was invented to allow the reader to pause and breathe, and to see a break in the ideas in the text.

Further inventions of punctuation included marks designed to show inflection, or pitch, tone, and volume. The fundamental punctuation marks for inflection are the question mark (?) and the exclamation point (!).

As we ask a question the pitch of our voice changes in different ways. Notice the fall of the pitch in your voice as you read the following question:

"What are you doing?"

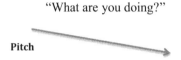

Pitch

Now notice the rise in the pitch of your voice as you ask a different kind of questions:

"Huh?"

Pitch

When teaching ELLs, it is important to remember that inflection in English is culturally determined. Consider the two questions above. How did you know to let the pitch of your voice fall for the first question and to rise for the second question? You probably just knew to change your pitch without thinking about it. It is something that you picked up from early childhood. However the use of pitch in a question is something that needs to be explicitly taught to ELLs.

Finally, the exclamation mark is a fascinating invention! According to Eveleth (2012), no one really knows where it came from. Some guess that it had Latin roots derived from a cryptic mash-up of the letters *OI* (!) as an expression of *JOY*! Surprisingly, the exclamation mark did not have a place on the keyboard until 1970. In earlier times, when bosses dictated to stenographers, they would say, "Bang!" to indicate the use of an exclamation mark in the written text of the letter. When a question mark and exclamation mark are combined (?! or !?), it is called an *interrobang*.

As the noise level of our society grows and social media expands, it seems that the exclamation mark is used more commonly than ever. There are even dedicated blog sites to document over-use of the exclamation mark such as "Excessive Exclamation!!" (http://excessiveexclamation.blogspot.com/).

Excessive exclamation, or volume, can be very unsettling to ELLs. Native English speakers rarely realize how loud they sound compared to speakers of other languages. In some Spanish-speaking countries such as Mexico, males only raise their voices in extreme panic or ecstatic situations. Imagine Mexican children, newly arrived in a classroom listening to the teacher use a loud "teacher voice" that connotes panic to their ears. The "teacher voice" sounds like screaming all day long, as if every sentence were punctuated with multiple exclamation marks!!! Insightful teachers of ELLs use volume judiciously. Consequently, let's use the exclamation mark when it is appropriately called for.

In sum, the classroom teacher develops the concepts of punctuation at the foundational level, by teaching usage in terms of three functions, namely pauses, breaks, and inflection. On a concrete level, ELLs practice breathing when they see a comma, semi-colon, or period. They learn that strong breaks in the text signify a new idea and they practice changes in pitch, tone, and volume when they use question marks and exclamation marks.

Print Concepts Activities

Performance Levels for Print Concepts

Foundational Reading Skills/ Performance Level Descriptors (PLDs)	Performance Level 1 Undeveloped	Performance Level 2 Approaching grade level	Performance Level 3 At Grade level
Print Concepts	Does not recognize print in English as significant. Does not track words from left to right. Names a few to no letters in the alphabet. No punctuation used.	Sees words as separated by spaces. Tracks words from left to right. Names upper and lower case alphabet. Identifies some ending punctuation.	Demonstrates understanding of the organization and basic features of print.

Kindergarten

Common Core State Standards for Print Concepts

CCSS.ELA-LITERACY.RF.K.1 (Anchor)
Demonstrate understanding of the organization and basic features of print.

CCSS.ELA-LITERACY.RF.K.1.A
Follow words from left to right, top to bottom, and page by page.
CCSS.ELA-LITERACY.RF.K.1.B
Recognize that spoken words are represented in written language by specific
    sequences of letters.
CCSS.ELA-LITERACY.RF.K.1.C
Understand that words are separated by spaces in print.
CCSS.ELA-LITERACY.RF.K.1.D
Recognize and name all upper- and lowercase letters of the alphabet.

Print Concepts Assessment

Before getting into activities related to Print Concepts, an assessment of initial orientation about print is needed. Cox (2013) provided an easy formative assessment
procedure that indicates left to right, top to bottom and word separation. The beauty
of this assessment is that it is easy to create, and developmentally speaking, young
children cannot fake that they know what to do. They either have a concept of print
orientation or they don't.

Directions:

1. Copy the following children's rhyme with large letters onto a large sheet of
    poster paper.

    One, two buckle my shoe
    Three, four shut the door
    Five, six pick up sticks
    Seven, eight lay them straight
    Nine, ten a big fat hen.

2. Read aloud the children's rhyme with the children as a group so that they all
    know what it says.
3. Point to each word as the group recites the poem, as a model.

4. One at a time, invite each of the children to do the same, lead the group by point to each word as they recite.
5. Note which students move their fingers from left to right and who points to the separate words as they recite. (ELLs with a different print orientation may begin at the top and move straight down, or from right to left. Young children without a concept of print orientation will move their finger along without pointing to separate words.)

Kindergarten Activities for Print Concepts

Activity at Performance Level 1

Ways to Teach Letter Shapes. Performance Level 1 ELLs need extra time to learn the letter shapes. In some cases, they may not be familiar with the same kind of script that we use in English. Some of those language groups include Arabic, Farsi, Korean, Mandarin, and many others. I recommend that teachers take a very tactile approach to teaching letter recognition. The following are some suggested ways to facilitate letter recognition using a tactile approach:

◆ Use a die-cut machine to make large letter shapes. Even better, die-cut letters using sandpaper. This increases the motivation for students to touch and feel the contours of each letter.
◆ Sand tray writing. Use a cookie sheet-like aluminum tray. Fill it with clean white sand. Encourage students to practice writing letter shapes with their finger in the sand. Supply students with letter and word cards to copy in the sand.
◆ Form letter shapes with "Wiki Stix." What are they? Picture multi-colored string that has been coated with a pliable waxy material. You can bend and mold the string to form virtually any shape, but it is particularly useful for letter formation (See: www.wikkistix.com/what_are_wikkistix.php).

Provide a table with the upper and lower case vowels and consonants. Review the vowels and consonants, and ask students to use a table like Table 4.1 as reference.

Table 4.1 Vowels and Consonants

Vowels and consonants UPPER and lower case	
V-vowels	**C-Consonants**
A a	B b
E e	C c
I i	D d
O o	
U u	F f
Y y	G g
	H h
	J j
	K k
	L l
	M m
	N n
	P p
	Q q
	R r
	S s
	V v
	W w
	X x
	Z z

Activity at Performance Level 2

Conduct Book Walks. Every time a teacher reads a book to young children, it is prudent to conduct a book walk. Book walks teach print orientation and develop print concepts through modeling.

Elements of a Book Walk are:

1. Display cover art, front and back
2. Ask predicting questions:
   - What do you think this is going to be about?
3. Identify: title, author, illustrator, publisher, and year
4. Ask the students to point to the title, author, illustrator, publisher, and year.
   - Make note of which students correctly point and those who have not developed book orientation as yet.
5. Walk through the story:
   - Read small segments
   - Note illustrations
   - Continue to ask predicting questions such as:
     - What do you think is happening?
6. Initiate a CWL activity (Adapted from *KWL* by Donna Ogle, 1986)
   - C= What clues do we have about this story?
   - W= What questions do you have about the story?
   - L= What did we learn from the story? (Wait until you finished the unit at the end of the semester.)
7. Read the entire story or in segments beginning the following class session with the students.

Activity at Performance Level 3

Make a Book. When students are engaged in creating a book from scratch, they actively learn book orientation and develop a clear understanding of print concepts. Making a book includes pasting text in order on to the book pages; illustrating each page, numbering pages in order; developing a title page that names the book, the author and illustrator. This is mounted with a front and back book cover with a taped spine.

Directions:

1. Select a simple text such as the children's rhyme above.
2. Print it onto letter-sized paper with each line on a separate row so that it can be cut up into sentence strips. Number each line of the rhyme.

> (1) One, two buckle my shoe
> (2) Three, four shut the door
> (3) Five, six pick up sticks
> (4) Seven, eight lay them straight
> (5) Nine, ten a big fat hen.

3. The book that the students will make will be six pages in length, including a title page plus a page for each of the five lines of the rhyme.
4. To keep it orderly, the first time you make a book with a group of Kindergarteners or first graders, give them the numbered sheet with the poem. Ask them to cut only the first line of the poem. When they show you the first sentence strip, cut correctly, give them a blank piece of paper and show them where to paste the sentence strip at the base of the page. (Check to see who pastes the sentence strip right side up for anecdotal information about print orientation.)
5. Ask the students to illustrate, "One, two buckle my shoe" on the page with the sentence strips pasted at the bottom.
6. Repeat steps #4 and #5 for each of the pages in the book.
7. Make a title page including a title, author (unknown), illustrator (child's name), and date. Include your school name, grade level, and room number (see example in Table 4.2).

Table 4.2 Sample Title Page

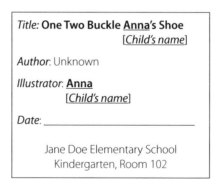

8. Combine all the pages in order (title page followed by the illustrated lines of the poem) and staple them together along the left-hand margin.
9. Number each page of the book in order.

10. Use two 9″×12″ pieces of heavy stock colored paper for the front and back cover of the book.
11. Staple the front and back covers of the book to the inside pages. Cover the stapled margin with book binding tape to make the spine of the book.
12. Ask the students to illustrate and write their name on the front cover of the book.

Tip: Keep the handmade books in a special section of the classroom library. Some teachers even glue in library pockets and maintain a checkout system for children to take their book home to read to family members. As students become familiar with book making, they can begin to create their own books with their own stories and poems.

1st Grade

Common Core State Standards for Print Concepts, First Grade

CCSS.ELA-LITERACY.RF.1.1
Demonstrate understanding of the organization and basic features of print.
CCSS.ELA-LITERACY.RF.1.1.A
Recognize the distinguishing features of a sentence (e.g., first word, capitalization, ending punctuation).

Activities at Performance Level 1

Language Experience Approach. The theoretical roots of language experience approaches (LEA) can be traced back to the Vygotsky's Zone of Proximal Development (Bruner, 1984; Halliday, Matthiessen, & Yang, 1999). Nessel and Jones (1981) advanced the idea of a language experience approach to reading instruction; and Moustafa (2014) reiterated the value of using a language experience approach with ELLs to help them meet the CCSS Foundational Skills in Reading. This approach uses the child's own words as the text for teaching reading. The teacher mediates the learning experience by writing down the child's words and calling attention to distinguishing features of the writing. In alignment with the CCSS, those distinguishing features of a sentence are the first word, capitalization, and punctuation.

Directions for Whole or Small Group LEA Instruction

1. Display a large sheet of poster-sized paper on the wall or on an easel.
2. Begin with a shared topic (special day, what did you learn in science lab?, a shared event like a field trip or concert, and so forth).
3. Ask an opening question:
   • What did we do yesterday. . . (at the zoo, or the Fire Department, etc.)?
   • Insist that the students respond with a sentence, not just a one word reply.

- If the ELL can only reply in one word, ask another student to use that word in a complete sentence.

4. Write the sentence down in large letters on the poster-sized paper so that all can see.
   - Use a green marking pen to write the first letter of the words that are capitalized (at the beginning of each sentence and proper nouns).
   - Use a red marking pen to highlight punctuation marks.

5. Talk about what you are doing as you write, such as saying, "Why did I write that letter in green? It is a capital letter. We begin each sentence with a capital letter." Or, "Notice the red period at the end of this sentence? That tells us to pause and breathe."

6. After writing a sentence, model how to read it, and then invite the class to read along with you.

7. Repeat steps 4–6 until you have approximately six sentences completed.

8. Read the entire text of the LEA chart story together as a class.

9. Split the class into partners. Ask the partners to take turns reading to each other.

10. Make a word-processed copy of the LEA chart story on regular letter-sized paper. Copy off a class set of the reduced-sized LEA story.

11. Ask each student to illustrate the story and take it home to read to a family member.

12. Inform family members that this will be a weekly homework assignment. Their child is to read an LEA story at home. The parents' role is to listen and ask questions, such as "What does this word mean?" "Can you tell me more about this event?" After listening and discussing, the parent must sign the story to confirm that they followed through with the homework.

Activities at Performance Level 2

LEA "How to" Big Book. To increase the level of complexity and engagement with print concepts, use language experience approach to create a collaborative big book.

Follow the Steps Provided Above for LEA With the Following Differences

1. Make the big book about how to do something. Here are some suggested topics:
   - How to make a nutritious breakfast.
   - How to change a flat tire on your bicycle.
   - How to write a letter to the President of the United States.
   - How to write a science experiment report.

2. Write enough sentences so that there are enough for the class (1 sentence for every two children because they will be working in pairs).

3. Negotiate the order of each sentence. Number them in the agreed-upon order. (In a collaborative composition, oftentimes the order of sentences needs to change to make logical sense of the text.)
4. Take scissors and slice up the LEA into individual sentence strips.
5. Divide the class into pairs, give one sentence to each pair of students, and give each pair a large sheet of paper as a page of the big book.
6. The responsibility of each pair of students is to do the following:
   • Rewrite the sentence clearly and accurately with punctuation on a large sheet of paper.
   • Illustrate the text.
   • Assign the correct page number to the page.
7. Gather together all the illustrated pages.
8. Staple them together along the left-hand margin.
9. Select some students to make a title page and to illustrate the cover of the book.
10. Bind the cover to the inside pages with a stapler followed by bookbinding tape.

Use the book as a resource for future reference. These "How to" big books are particularly helpful for struggling students when they cover topics such as how to write a letter or how to complete a science report.

Consider all the print concepts that are involved in making a book. To extend the experience, divide the class into work groups of 4–6 students. Each group gets a "How to" topic to develop into a big book. Assign a student to be managing editor. The managing editor is the liaison between the group and you as teacher in the development of the book. If the group needs materials, for example, they must work through the managing editor. This makes for efficient oversight of multiple groups functioning at the same time.

Activities at Performance Level 3

LEA Character Study. Integrate Common Core Standards for Literary Texts with Foundational Skills by conducting a collaborative character study with LEA.

1. Display a poster-sized sheet of paper with a drawing of a selected character in a literary work the class is currently reading.
2. Provide each student with a letter-size paper with a space in the middle to draw a picture of the same literary character.
   • There is a myriad of Google images of line art figures for character study; but I prefer to have students draw free hand.
3. Follow the above steps for LEA to draft the students' words and ideas about the character.

4. Write the sentences around the drawing of the character, so that it is surrounded with observations that the students made about the character.
5. Ask for details about the character such as descriptions of appearance, actions, and motivations.
   - Keep the literary text at the ready to ask students "where did you see that detail in the story?" "Is that what the author meant to write?"
6. Highlight writing conventions of capitalization, punctuation, and spelling.
   - With new or difficult words, ask students to help you spell them correctly.
7. While the teacher is writing sentences on the display paper, students are also writing on their reduced-sized individual character study sheets.
8. An extension of this activity is to use a form of a Venn Diagram to compare and contrast competing characters in one or more literary texts.

References

Bruner, J. (1984). Vygotsky's zone of proximal development: The hidden agenda. *New Directions for Child and Adolescent Development*, (23), 93–97.

Chappell, W., & Bringhurst, R. (1970/1990). *A short history of the printed word*. (2nd Ed.). Vancouver, BC: Hartley & Marks Publishers.

Cox, C. (2013). *Teaching language arts: A response-centered, child-centered approach*. Boston: Allyn & Bacon, Pearson Education.

Eveleth, R. (August 9, 2012). The history of the exclamation point: Everyone likes to complain that we are using too many exclamation points these days. Here's where the punctuation came from. *Smithsonian.com*. www.smithsonianmag.com/smart-news/the-history-of-the-exclamation-point-16445416/?no-ist

Gentry, R. (2010). *Raising confident readers*. Boston, MA: Da Capo Press.

Halliday, M.A.K., Matthiessen, C.M., & Yang, X. (1999). *Construing experience through meaning: A language-based approach to cognition*. London: Cassell.

Healy, J. (1990). *The history of the alphabet*. Los Angeles: University of California Press.

Jonson, B. & Gifford, W. (1903). *The works of Ben Jonson, Volume III*. London: Ballantyne, Hanson, & Co.

Moustafa, M. (2014). Improving the Common Core's Foundational Skills in Reading, K–2. *The California Reader*, 48(1), 11–19.

Nessel, D.D., & Jones, M.B. (1981). *The language-experience approach to reading: A handbook for teachers*. New York: Teachers College Press.

Ogle, D.M. (1986). KWL: A teaching model that develops active reading of expository text. *The Reading Teacher*, 39(6), 564–570.

Saenger, P. (1997). *The space between words: The origins of silent reading*. Santa Clara, CA: Stanford University Press.

5

Phonological Awareness
Kindergarten–Grade 1

In the previous chapter we discussed print concepts, which essentially means seeing print as significant and having a clear orientation of its structure and use. It is a visual developmental process. Phonological awareness, by contrast, is an auditory and an oral developmental process. It is receptive and expressive in nature, developing awareness and understanding of spoken words, and recognizing and pronouncing syllables/sounds in English.

With the Common Core phonological awareness is addressed only in kindergarten and 1st-grade standards. According to CCSS, there are four components to Phonemic Awareness:

1. Distinguishing vowel sounds.
2. Orally blending sounds, including consonant blends.
3. Isolating and orally pronouncing initial, medial vowel, and final sounds in words.
4. Segmenting words into a sequence of individual sounds.

For an English language learner, developing phonological awareness in a second language cannot be done apart from understanding and meaningful usage of the language. Awareness marks a progression in development from recognizing noises to distinguishing sounds to understanding messages and interpreting expressions. Krashen (1982, 1985) described two aspects of gaining knowledge about a language: language learning and language acquisition. Language learning is the analytical side of gaining knowledge about a language. We learn about a language when we break it down into parts, analyze the structure, and classify its sounds. Language acquisition is the usage side of gaining knowledge about a language. Language acquisition is subconscious and takes place involuntarily as we understand the messages being expressed in meaningfully communicative contexts.

Interestingly, we can analyze or learn about a language, such as Spanish, by describing the number of vowel sounds, but that knowledge is insufficient to understand and produce meaningful messages in Spanish. In contrast, native speakers of any language rarely analyze how they use their own language as they speak because it was subconsciously acquired as they grew up communicating with others in meaningful ways. The challenge for classroom teachers of ELLs, therefore, is to bring together the analysis of a language with meaningful messages so that awareness and understanding are developed together for appropriate application in English.

Explicit instruction for phonological awareness is more on the language learning side of instruction. Note the verbs used to describe the actions of phonological awareness: distinguish, blend, isolate, pronounce, and segment. Analyzing a language, though very interesting, is an abstract exercise and quite different from using the language to receive messages and express oneself. Native English speakers don't stop in mid-speech to analyze sounds into initial, medial, or final position in a word—they'd never get through talking about their day if they did. However, as teachers, we appropriately pause to ask students to stop and analyze specific words so that their receptive understanding and usage develop. Additionally, teachers assess phonological awareness as they observe to what degree their students are distinguishing vowel sounds, blending consonants, isolating and orally pronouncing sounds in various word positions (initial, medial, final), and segmenting words into a sequence of sounds appropriately.

As stated earlier in Chapter 3, seeing how words, syllables, and sounds are formed in the mouth helps English learners hear the sounds. Although this may seem counter-intuitive, think back to a time as a teacher when you found yourself repeating the same word over and over to a student only to hear him or her repeat back something quite different. The student repeated what s/he heard and understood, not necessarily what was said. For example, you can say the word *because* to a Spanish speaker; but that Spanish speaker will hear /*picuz*/. They will not hear the /b-/, in initial position, they will hear a /p-/. No matter how many times you repeat it clearly and slowly, the initial sound will not be recognized until that Spanish speaker sees and feels the difference of how the /b-/ is formed in the mouth in English.

Figure 5.1 Trapezoidal Vowel Chart

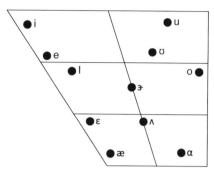

The reason that the native Spanish speaker does not distinguishing the two sounds is that, in Spanish, the difference virtually does not exist, or is minimally perceptible; the difference in English, however, is more dramatic. It is the puff of air that is pushed out with the /p-/ versus the buzz that takes place with the /b-/. Therefore, the most efficient way to help an ELL in this case with phonological awareness is to have them place a hand on their throat to feel the buzz as they say /b-/ and in contrast to hold a strip of paper in front of their lips as they push out a /p-/ to see the air push the paper aside.

A helpful visual is to see a vowel chart that shows where vowel sounds in the English language are formed in the mouth. This dramatically increases phonemic awareness. Although there are as many as 20 vowel sounds in English, note how vowels can be charted relative to their position in the mouth with a trapezoidal vowel chart (Figure 5.1). Wikipedia provides an interactive vowel chart that includes digitized audio pronunciation for every position in the mouth (http://en.wikipedia.org/wiki/IPA_vowel_chart_with_audio).

After seeing how the teacher forms specific blends in the mouth, including how to position the tongue and lips, the ELL can look at their own formation of blends looking at their mouths in the mirror.

Phonological Awareness Activities

The Performance Level Descriptors for Phonological Awareness establish a range from Level 1, where the ELL is essentially silent and may not recognize meaningful sounds in English, to Level 3, where the ELL is operating at grade level expectancy in understanding spoken words, and recognizing syllables and phonemes. Level 2 is a transitional phase when the ELL demonstrates some oral comprehension. It is immediately discernable when the ELL is able to respond to simple oral directions. For oral language development strategies related to the Common Core Listening and Speaking Standards, see Helping English Language Learners Meet the Common Core (Boyd-Batstone, 2013).

Performance Levels for Phonological Awareness

Foundational Reading Skills/ Performance Level Descriptors (PLDs)	Performance Level 1 Undeveloped foundational skills	Performance Level 2 Developing grade level foundational skills	Performance Level 3 Grade level foundational skills
Phonological Awareness	Remains silent. Does not comprehend simple spoken words. Does not distinguish syllables and individual sounds in words.	Comprehends simple words and sentences. Follows oral directions. Isolates and pronounces the initial, medial vowel, and final sounds (phonemes) in three-phoneme (consonant-vowel-consonant, or CVC) words.	Demonstrates understanding of spoken words, syllables, and sounds (phonemes).

Kindergarten

Common Core State Standards for Phonological Awareness

Phonological Awareness:

CCSS.ELA-LITERACY.RF.K.2
Demonstrate understanding of spoken words, syllables, and sounds (phonemes).
CCSS.ELA-LITERACY.RF.K.2.A
Recognize and produce rhyming words.
CCSS.ELA-LITERACY.RF.K.2.B
Count, pronounce, blend, and segment syllables in spoken words.
CCSS.ELA-LITERACY.RF.K.2.C
Blend and segment onsets and rimes of single-syllable spoken words.
CCSS.ELA-LITERACY.RF.K.2.D
Isolate and pronounce the initial, medial vowel, and final sounds (phonemes) in three-phoneme (consonant-vowel-consonant, or CVC) words. (This does not include CVCs ending with /l/, /r/, or /x/.)
CCSS.ELA-LITERACY.RF.K.2.E
Add or substitute individual sounds (phonemes) in simple, one-syllable words to make new words.

Activities for Performance Level 1

Total Physical Response. When ELLs are in that silent stage, they are actively listening to grasp something meaningful. Much of what they hear is indiscernible noise. I like to show the teacher candidates at my university a video of kindergarten classroom instruction in Mandarin from Beijing, China. I ask the students to imagine themselves as a newly arrived kindergarten student in the class. I ask them to look for meaningful moments in the class and what the teacher did to help them understand the lesson. For the most part, they don't understand the lesson because they are at that silent stage of language development in Mandarin. However, there are times when the lesson becomes more understandable because the teacher shows visuals and actively involves the students in meaningful gestures.

In oral language development, the use of Total Physical Response (TPR) (Asher, 1969) has proven to be an effective strategy. Total Physical Response involves modeling a physical movement or meaningful gesture as you teach the word for that action. If you want to teach the word "catch," you don't begin with an abstract word card; you get a sponge-ball, toss it in the air and say "catch" as you grasp hold of the ball. You repeat the action and only this time you toss the ball to a student and say, "catch."

You move ELLs from receptive to oral language to reading print by acting out those physical actions as numbered and written commands. The following TPR Chart (Table 5.1) shows the extent of written language that can be comprehended by ELLs at Level 1, who are silent.

Table 5.1 TPR Chart

1.	**Touch** your nose.
2.	**Reach** for the sky.
3.	**Smile** a big smile.
4.	**Clap** your hands together.

The simple commands shown in that table are read aloud and modeled by the teacher. Numbering the commands helps ELLs follow the written language as they act out the oral commands. Notice that each action verb is written in command form at the beginning of the sentence. The TPR commands are not written like dictionary definitions, they convey meaning when the appropriate action accompanies the text.

Now apply TPR to a Mother Goose (n.d.) rhyme:

Cross Patch, **lift** the latch,
Sit by the fire and **spin**;
Take a cup, and **drink** it up,
Then **call** your neighbors in.

Selecting a rhyme like the one above, with multiple verbs in command form, permits reading instruction to Level 1 ELLs using a literary work by acting out the various actions in the poem.

Another application of TPR is to establish an imaginary scenario where the ELLs are role-playing a character in the story. Create a TPR Chart with numbered commands that recreate the narrative of part of a story. For example, ask the students to imagine that they are Peter Rabbit in Beatrix Potter's (1902) famous story. Use the following TPR Chart (Table 5.2) to give meaning to the story:

Table 5.2 TPR Applied to a Story

TPR chart	
1.	**Open** the gate to McGregor's garden.
2.	**Dig** up a carrot.
3.	**Nibble** the tip of the carrot.
4.	**Look** behind you! Here comes Mr. McGregor.
5.	**Jump** into the watering can.
6.	**Sneeze** from the chill.
7.	**Crawl** under the gate.
8.	**Run** home.
9.	**Crawl** into bed.
10.	**Drink** chamomile tea.

Providing a sequence of commands that follow the text of the story includes silent ELLs into the text of the story. Take note that some of the commands would become even more meaningful if props were provided. In the above TPR chart, the teacher can supply the following materials as props:

◆ A backdrop with a picture of the gate to the garden
◆ Brown paper with rows drawn in to simulate garden rows
◆ Carrots
◆ Use a hula hoop to create an imaginary watering can to jump into
◆ Use a sheet or a blanket for a bed
◆ A toy tea set for the chamomile tea

Activities for Performance Level 2

Song and Word Play. When the children's folk singer Raffi (1985) recorded the traditional song, "I like to eat apples and bananas," it was an international success because of the fun word play involved. For a reminder, the song is a simple repetition of "I like to eat, eat, eat apples and bananas." The brilliance of the song is that it inserts a vowel in each syllable of apples and bananas with each verse. I recommend that teachers continue to play with the song and encourage their students to play with the words of the song too. Here is one such example of playing with the song lyrics:

I like to eat, eat, eat
I like to eat tacos and burritos.
A— I like to Ayt, Ayt, Ayt; I like to Ayt tacas and barratas.
E— I like to EEt, EEt, EEt; I like to EEt teckes end berretes.
I— I like to IYt, IYt, IYt; I like to Iyt tiquis ind birritis.
O— I like to Oat, Oat, Oat; I like to Oat tocos ond borrotos.
U— I like to UUt, UUt, UUt; I like to Uut tucus und burrutus.

Invite the students to substitute other silly combinations of things to eat like "butter on my green beans" or even "monsters in the morning." It follows a simple syllable count pattern of 2=apples/1=and/3=bananas. You can create a word bank to help students come up with combinations (see Table 5.3). Students simply pick one word or phrase from each column, but make sure that the preposition or conjunction in the middle makes sense:

Table 5.3 Word Bank

2 Syllables	1 Syllable	3 Syllables
Tacos	And	Burritos
Butter	On	My green beans
Pickles	In	Spaghetti
Jelly	With	Big doughnuts
Meatballs		Some ketchup
Oatmeal		Brown sugar
Monsters		The morning

A Word of CAUTION: Avoid using "ice cream," or any other combination that may result in singing something unexpectedly rude sounding when the vowels are substituted. If you don't get what I am warning you about, substitute the vowels in "ice cream" with the letter "A," then say it out loud to nobody. You've been forewarned.

Culturally Relevant Texts and Primary Language Support. There is a traditional Mexican folksong in Spanish that uses the same vowel substitution technique, but it has a Day of the Dead theme about two skeletons, a daughter and her mother. It is sung in schools and is even part of the curriculum, *Dirección Principal de Educación Primaria* (2007). See Table 5.4.

Mexican Folksong: "Estaba la Calavera"

Estaba la calavera
Sentada en una butaca
Vino la madre y dijo,
"¡Hija! ¿Por qué estas tan flaca?"

Table 5.4 Translation and Poetic Rendering of Mexican Folksong

Literal translation	Poetic rendering
There was a little girl skeleton	A skeleton girl was sitting
Sitting on a casket	Upon an empty casket;
Her mother came by and said,	When her mother came by
"Daughter! Why are you so skinny?"	She cried out, "Oh my!"
	You look like an empty basket!

(Translations by Paul Boyd-Batstone)

Mexican Folksong: "Estaba la Calavera"

Estaba la calavera
Sentada en una butaca
Vino la madre y dijo,
"¡Hija! ¿Por qué estas tan flaca?"

A

Astaba la calavara
Santada an ana bataca
Vana la madra a daja,
"¡Haja! ¿Par qué astas tan flaca?"

E

Estebe le quelevere
Sentede en ene beteque
Vene le medre e deje,
"¡Heje! ¿Per qué estes ten fleque?"

(And so forth through the five vowels: A, E, I, O, and U)

The humor in the Mexican folksong is morbidly funny—a mother skeleton wondering why her daughter skeleton has no meat on her bones. Some families from Mexico don't celebrate Day of the Dead for personal and religious reasons, so check with them before employing this song. It also functions as a Halloween-type song in English.

English Translation of the Mexican Folksong. Now are you up for the challenge of vowel substitution with this translated folksong? Have fun chanting the words. Laugh and enjoy the substitutions. Instructionally, pay attention to the position of your mouth as you say the words. This will help give guidance to ELLs as to how to articulate the sounds in English.

English Version: "A Skeleton Girl" by Paul Boyd-Batstone

A skeleton girl was sitting
Upon an empty casket;
When her mother came by
She cried out, "Oh my!"
You look like an empty basket!

A

A skalatan garl was sattang
Apan an ampta caskat;
Whan har mathar came ba
Sha crad at, "Ah ma!"
Ya lak lake an ampta baskat!

E

E skeleten gerl wes setteng
Epen en empty kesket;
When her mether keme be
She cred et, "Eh me!"
Ye lek leke an empte besket!

I

> I skilitin girl wis sitting
> Ipin in impti kiskit;
> Whin hir mithir kime bi
> Shi crid it, "Ih mi!"
> Yi lik like in impti biskit!

O

> O skoloton gorl wos sottong
> Opon on ompto koskot;
> Whon hor mothor kome bo
> Sho crod ot, "Oh mo!"
> Yo lok loke on ompto boskot!

U

> U skulutun gurl wus suttung
> Upun un umptu kuskut;
> Whun hur muthur cume bu
> Shu crud ut, "Uh mu!"
> Yu luk luke un umptu buskut!

Activities for Performance Level 3

Pocket Mirrors and Pronunciation. Teachers can waste time and energy having ELLs repeat sounds in whole group settings or simply telling an ELL to "sound it out." As pointed out earlier, it might seem counter-intuitive, but having ELLs see how to form their mouths to make sounds is much more helpful and efficient instructionally with teaching phonemes.

Table 5.5 is a chart that displays 20 different vowel utterances in English. In addition, there is a column for how to form the sound in the mouth, words that use that sound, and letter combinations used to write the sounds.

Provide ELLs with a pocket mirror so that they can see their own mouths as they form the sounds. In the age of smart phones, have them take "selfies" of their mouths forming the sounds correctly. Note that some of the vowel digraphs and r-controlled vowels use two positions in the mouth, for example: /oi/ Begin with rounded lips and finish with a smile.

Table 5.5 Forming Vowel Sounds

Vowel sound	Mouth position	Words with the same vowel sound	Letter combinations
/ă/	Open the mouth; Smile	cat	a
/ā/	Stretch open the mouth	make, rain, play, great, baby, eight, vein, they	a/e, ai, ay, ea,-y, eigh, ei, ey
/ē/	Stretch open the mouth; Smile	see, these, me, eat, key, happy, chief, either	ee, e/e,-e, ea, ey,-y, ie, ei
/ĕ/	Slight stretch open; Drop the chin	bed, breath	e, ea
/ĭ/	Stretch lips across the teeth	sit, gym	i, y
/ī/	Open the mouth; Drop the jaw	time, pie, cry, right, rifle	i_e, ie,-y, igh,-i
/aw/	Drop the jaw outward	father, saw, pause, call, water, cough	a, aw, au, all, wa, ough
/ŏ/	Open the mouth; Use the throat	fox, swap, palm	o, wa, al
/ō/	Round the lips; Use the throat	vote, boat, toe, snow, open	o_e, oa, oe, ow, o-
/oi/	Begin with rounded lips; Finish with a smile	boil, boy	oi, oy
/oo/	Round lips slightly	took, put, could	oo, u, ou
/ow/	Drop jaw; Finish with lip rounding	out, cow	ou, ow
/ŭ/	Drop jaw; Use the throat	cup, cover, flood, tough	u, o, oo, ou
/ū/ [oo]	Round the lips forward	moo, tube, blue, chew, suit, soup	oo, u_e, ue, ew, ui, ou
/y//ū/	Stretch lips across the teeth; Finish with lip rounding	use, few, cute	u, ew, u_e

(Continued)

Table 5.5 (Continued)

Vowel sound	Mouth position	Words with the same vowel sound	Letter combinations
R-controlled vowel sounds			
/ar/	Open mouth; Finish with dropping jaw to the side	cart	ar
/er/	Slight open mouth; Finish with dropping jaw to the side	her, fur, sir	er, ur, ir
/ir/	Stretch lips across teeth; Finish with dropping jaw to the side	chirp	ir
/or/	Drop jaw open; Finish with dropping jaw to the side	sort	or
/ur/	Round the lips forward; Finish with dropping jaw to the side	slurp	ur

1st Grade

Common Core State Standards for Phonological Awareness

Phonological Awareness:

CCSS.ELA-LITERACY.RF.1.2
Demonstrate understanding of spoken words, syllables, and sounds (phonemes).
CCSS.ELA-LITERACY.RF.1.2.A
Distinguish long from short vowel sounds in spoken single-syllable words.
CCSS.ELA-LITERACY.RF.1.2.B
Orally produce single-syllable words by blending sounds (phonemes), including
    consonant blends.
CCSS.ELA-LITERACY.RF.1.2.C
Isolate and pronounce initial, medial vowel, and final sounds (phonemes) in
    spoken single-syllable words.
CCSS.ELA-LITERACY.RF.1.2.D

Segment spoken single-syllable words into their complete sequence of individual
sounds (phonemes).

Activities for Performance Level 1

Make an Acrostic With Your Name. Using a child's name to teach initial literacy taps into a learning space that is close to the heart. Provide each student with a two column name card that includes the child's name written in block letters in the left-hand column and a longer space on the write to select words. Prepare a set of cards that provide descriptive words from every letter of the alphabet. Ask the students to find a word with the beginning letter matching a letter from their name. Place the matching initial sound word card next to the appropriate letter of their name (Table 5.6).

Table 5.6 Name Acrostic (Template and Completed Version)

M	
E	
L	
I	

(Continued)

Table 5.6 (Continued)

N	
A	
M	MARVEL
E	EXTRA NICE
L	LITTLE
I	INTELLIGENT
N	NEAT
A	ABLE

Activities for Performance Level 2

Phoneme Identity, Isolation, Blending, Segmentation. Analysis follows exploration. The previous activities in this section involved exploring phonemes through word play in song, chanting silly words, and developing an awareness of how to form sounds in the mouth with pocket mirrors and a phoneme chart. This next set of activities involves language analysis of phonemes. There is a progression involved of identifying individual phonemes, isolating phonemes, blending phonemes, and segmenting words into phonemes. These types of activities build understanding of the language, but they do not build fluency.

I'll use the analogy of how a kid uses a bicycle. Most of the time he rides a bicycle as he fluidly glides down the street; however, there are times when he takes the bicycle apart to learn how it works. When all the parts to the bicycle are lying on the floor, it doesn't ride very well; but as the kid puts the bike back together, he learns how it works. The same applies to phoneme analysis, when all the parts of a word are spread across the child's desk it is difficult to use the words fluently. When they are put back together, the child learns how the language works. So fluent reading is developed in other ways such as reading stories, singing songs, reciting poetry, posing an argument, perusing the news, and giving presentations. With these activities, we slow down to examine and analyze phonemes. (The following activities are taken from the CCSS Appendix-B.)

Phoneme Identity

Say the sound that begins these words. What is your mouth doing when you make that sound?

◆ milk, mouth, monster /m/: The lips are together, and the sound goes through the nose.
◆ thick, thimble, thank /th/: The tongue is between the teeth, and a hissy sound is produced.
◆ octopus, otter, opposite /o/: The mouth is wide open, and we can sing that sound.

Phoneme Isolation

What is the first speech sound in this word?

◆ ship /sh/
◆ van /v/
◆ king /k/
◆ echo /e/

What is the last speech sound in this word?

◆ comb /m/
◆ sink /k/
◆ rag /g/
◆ go /o/

Phoneme Blending (Spoken Language)

Blend the sounds to make a word:
(Provide these sounds slowly.)

◆ /s/ /ay/ say
◆ /ou/ /t/ out
◆ /sh/ /ar/ /k/ shark
◆ /p/ /o/ /s/ /t/ post

Phoneme Segmentation (Spoken Language)

Say each sound as you move a chip onto a line or sound box:

◆ no /n/ /o/
◆ rag /r/ /a/ /g/
◆ socks /s/ /o/ /k/ /s/
◆ float /f/ /l/ /oa/ /t/

Activities for Performance Level 3

Syllable Counting With Environmental Print. Using environmental print to teach initial reading skills employs words and texts that are part of the everyday lives of your students. This is particularly helpful for ELLs because the words are naturally embedded in rich context.

There are multiple ways to utilize environment print such as capturing labels from grocery store items. Cut out grocery labels. Lay them on the students' desks. Give students a cup of dried and painted lima beans to use as counting chips. Say the words on the labels and count the syllables with the counting chips. Then have the students record the word onto the appropriate column in chart like Table 5.7.

Table 5.7 Sorting Words By Number of Syllables

1 Syllable ✪	2 Syllables ✪✪	3 Syllables ✪✪✪
Soap	Toothpaste	Detergent
Box	Pickles	Cereal
Wheat	Cookies	
Oats		
Milk		

Another way to count syllables using environmental print is to conduct a word walk through the neighborhood. Use the above table and clip it to a piece of thick cardboard for backing. As you come across words on signs along the way, stop and analyze the words you find. Count the syllables and record the words in the syllable table.

References

Asher, J.J. (1969). The total physical response approach to second language learning. *The Modern Language Journal*, 53(1), 3–17.

Boyd-Batstone, P. (2013). *Helping English language learners meet the Common Core: Assessment and Instructional Strategies K–12*. New York: Eye on Education/Routledge.

Cavoukian, Raffi (1985). I like to eat apples and bananas. *One Light, One Sun*. www.raffinews.com/store/childrens-music/one-light-one-sun#. VAaEumRdWRM

Krashen, S. (1982). *Principles and practice in second language acquisition*. Pergamon: Oxford.

Krashen, S.D. (1985). *The input hypothesis: Issues and implications*. London: Longman.

Mother Goose or the Old Nursery Rhymes (n.d.). *The Project Gutenberg*. www.gutenberg.org/files/23794/23794-h/23794-h.htm#Page_19

Ocho Poemitas: Material para el alumno. (2007). Dirección Provincial de Educación Primaria. http://servicios2.abc.gov.ar/lainstitucion/sistema educativo/educprimaria/areascurriculares/lengua/practicas_nro_8_poemitas_material_para_el_alumno.pdf

Potter, B. (1902). *The tale of Peter Rabbit*. London: Fredrick Warne & Co.

6

Phonics and Word Recognition
Kindergarten–Grade 5

In the Common Core Standards, phonics and word recognition are treated as a single category, and rightly so. They support each other. Over the years, phonics has taken on a very large role in foundational reading instruction and some might say too large a role due to huge commercial interests. That issue will not be addressed in this chapter, however. The purpose of this chapter is to discuss and demonstrate phonics and word recognition instructional practice that is meaningful for English language learners in relation to specific Common Core Foundational Reading Standards.

One way to approach phonics and word recognition is to think of them as two sides to the same coin. One side is auditory; the other is visual. Phonics instruction focuses on sound-symbol relationships, while word recognition focuses on identifying visual patterns, families of words, and irregular constructions.

Conventional thinking would tell us that the auditory side develops first; however, with ELLs they will tend to first recognize words and patterns visually before they acquire sound-symbol relationships. To illustrate my point, think of yourself looking at a menu in a French restaurant, you may recognize *coq au vin* as chicken in wine sauce, but not necessarily know how to pronounce it like a French native. I've spoken with proficient ELLs who never quite mastered the /æ/ "uh" sound, or schwa, in English. The sounds follow the visual recognition; but neither auditory, nor visual representations make sense until they are presented in meaningful ways.

In the following discussions of phonics and word recognition, I recommend that we help ELLs with phonics and word recognition when we provide meaningful instruction first. Isolated sounds can be just as abstract and meaningless as isolated word cards void of contextual support. Historically, phonics and word recognition have been like competitive siblings, each vying for dominant time in reading instruction. Let's keep in mind that phonics and word recognition are foundational skills, but they are not the ultimate goal of reading instruction. Independent, skilled reading for purpose and meaning is the goal. From the perspective of ELLs, they are looking to make sense of the abstract thing called English. Let's do what we can to make it meaningful first and then respond to their auditory and visual instructional needs.

Phonics

According to Timothy Shanahan (2006), a member of the National Reading Panel and an expert panelist who worked to develop the Common Core Standards, phonics instruction can be defined as follows:

> Phonics instruction teaches students to use the relationship between letters and sounds to translate printed text into pronunciation. It includes the teaching of letter sounds, how complex spelling patterns are pronounced, and how to use this information to decode or sound out words. (p. 11)

The Report of the National Reading Panel (NRP/NICHD, 2000) reviewed the findings of 38 research studies on phonics instruction. In particular, the impact of two different approaches to phonics instruction was examined, *synthetic* and *analytic*. Although the synthetic approach, when used systematically on a daily basis, showed stronger impact with certain populations, the differences were not found to be statistically significant. Additionally, the NRP did not look at studies of phonics instruction with English language learners.

Synthetic or Analytic Phonics?

To briefly illustrate how the approaches differ, a teacher of *synthetic*, or explicit, phonics would set aside time each day to teach how to pronounce individual letter sounds and blends such as /bl-/. More often than not, the instruction would be drawn from a commercial program that systematically addressed a full range of phonics rules. In contrast, a teacher of *analytic*, or more contextualized, phonics would pause during a reading lesson to provide an in-the-moment mini-lesson, asking students to analyze /bl-/ as it appeared in a passage with the words *bl*ue, *bl*ack, and *bl*ouse.

In the *synthetic* approach, daily explicit instruction of letter sounds and blends may or may not be connected to what students are reading or writing on a particular day; while the *analytical* approach would depend on the context of the students' daily reading and writing activities. Further, the synthetic approach would tend to emphasize pronunciation of isolated sounds and words; whereas the analytical approach would tend to emphasize word recognition, in context, along with pronunciation.

Before we discuss the relative merits and limitations of the above approaches, it is important to consider a particular, rather quiet, finding of the NRP with regard to the impact of phonics instruction. There appeared to be a much greater impact of systematic phonic instruction with kindergarten and first grade English-speaking children. The reason was that their oral language vocabulary was in advance of their reading/writing vocabulary. Thus the children were learning to recognize in print many of the words that they already knew orally. Hence the impact of synthetic versus analytic approaches was minimal because they already knew the words. In later grades, where the written language was much better known by the children, phonics instruction had very limited impact regardless of approach.

This quiet finding is important to understanding one key difference between teaching phonics and word recognition to native English speakers and ELLs. That key difference is the role of oral language development in foundational reading instruction. Native English speakers at the kindergarten level come to phonics instruction with five years of English oral language development already in place. ELLs in contrast, at the beginning stages of language development, do not have that essential oral language in English to know the words they are being asked to pronounce without prior vocabulary instruction. Therefore, simply "sounding out" words may not be very meaningful for an ELL.

To get a feel for what an ELL might experience, try this activity on yourself: Find a foreign language radio station. Listen to the announcers, their accents, cadence, and pronunciation of words. Then try to mimic their speaking. Depending on the sensitivity of your ear, you may very well approximate their sounds. But then try to figure out what you just tried to mimic. It is just a bunch of sounds. You get the idea that mouthing a collection of sounds is not communicative and not meaningful. A primary goal with ELLs is to provide meaning and meaningful contexts for instruction in all scenarios and especially at the foundational level of reading.

Benefits and Limitations of Phonics Instruction

Shanahan (2006) pointed out that daily instruction in phonics was found to be beneficial among English speakers at early grades and with struggling readers to a certain extent. *Synthetic*, explicit phonics instruction provided a routine of practice in letter and blend recognition and pronunciation. It also helped students recognize spelling patterns. What made a difference was the systematic nature of instruction regardless of approach. Commercial phonics programs are *synthetic* and attempt to provide a systematic overview of letter sounds and blends for decoding purposes.

Limitations of *synthetic* phonics instruction include the ineffectual nature of teaching isolated letter sounds. Consonants in English tend to be associated with a vowel sound, or a schwa /æ/ "uh" sound. Therefore the isolated consonant sounds /*cuh*/ /ă/ /*tuh*/ do not correspond to how the word "CAT" actually sounds. An English speaker would already know the word "CAT" orally and so the isolated sounds of the letters might not be so confounding. However, the isolation of letter sounds can be profoundly confusing to English learners who would not see or hear the relationship of the sounds of the letters to the word.

Furthermore, although commercial phonics programs establish a systematic overview of phonics, they can be costly and over-reaching in their claims. Many administrators gladly pay the price for commercial phonics programs because they provide a systematic program of instruction, especially to novice teachers. Commercial phonics programs function as an organizer of instruction; however their use can have the effect of supplanting comprehensive reading instruction. Some novice teachers use their entire reading instructional time to teach phonics at the expense of quality time spent reading, developing vocabulary, discussing ideas, and writing about reading.

Consider also that commercial phonics programs provide readers, or "decodable texts" at considerable expense. The purpose of the decodable texts is to provide students with something to read that concentrates on particular sounds. For example, a brief story will be constructed around a sound, such as /n/. (Here's a decodable text that I made up: *Nick* and *Ned never need noodles.*) Apart from the collection of words using /n/ in a sentence, the text itself is not very compelling. The significance of the text is secondary to the collection of emphasized sounds. An important finding from the NRP was that the use of decodable texts had no positive impact on reading instruction. In addition, the practice of reading decodable texts was not found to benefit reading comprehension.

In comparison, *analytic*, or more contextualized phonics instruction, has been found to be meaningful for English language learners in particular (Moustafa, 2002). Analyzing letters, blends, and sounds in the context of daily reading instruction develops word recognition at the same time as pronunciation. Analyzing words in context allows the teacher the opportunity to show how words are used, to compare multiple examples of usage, and to increase retention because the words are connected to the context of a story, or a text. In this approach, the teacher also asks students to provide examples of given letters or blends from their own personal experiences. For example, teachers using this approach will ask students to bring examples from home, or to draw a picture of something from their neighborhood that uses the /bl-/ sound. *Analytic* phonics instruction also works hand-in-glove with vocabulary instruction for ELLs. As new vocabulary is introduced, students are asked to analyze its make-up and sound, and to compare it other examples in their reading and writing.

The limitations of *analytic* phonics instruction include the challenge of providing a comprehensive, rather than sporadic, plan of instruction. Teachers who only engage in on-the-spot analysis of letters and words may risk not providing their students with a complete range of phonics skills. Therefore it is incumbent upon teachers who rely on *analytic* phonics instruction to systematically plan to address the full range of phonics within their reading instruction. This means identifying in unit planning which letters and blends will be addressed over the course of the instructional period.

Therefore, both approaches have their benefits and limitations. Teachers who base their practice on research-based recommended practices should do the following:

Positive Practices

- Provide daily phonics and word recognition instruction.
- Provide meaningful contexts for instruction.
- Utilize sample words from the context of daily reading.
- Provide oral language support with vividly illustrated words and texts.
- Teach vocabulary using all the senses.
- Actively engage students in finding examples of word structures in their own neighborhoods.

Negative Practices

- Avoid teaching mimicking or mouthing sounds in isolation.
- Reduce the use of decodable texts.

Word Recognition

While phonics is associated with auditory aspects of reading, word recognition is the visual side. Visually recognizing words is particularly germane to learning to read in English because of the numerous inconsistencies of spelling. This is due to the hybrid nature of the language and to the fact that languages creatively evolve over time. English is a language that draws mostly from Latin roots, and many other sources including Greek, Arabic, Teutonic words, and a collection of Middle English single syllable words like "pig" and "cow."

There are irregularities and variations in English that require visual recognition over auditory discrimination. They manifest exceptions to virtually every phonics-based rule. For example "though" and "cough" and "hiccough" pose problems for auditory perception. Additionally with names: for example, my daughter is named "Kathryn," but she must endure having her name misspelled as Katharine, Katherin, Katherynn, Kathrynn, Katherynne, Kathrynne, Catherine, Cathryn, Catharine, Catherin, Catherynn, Cathrynn, Catherynne, or Cathryne. I've lost count of the variations.

Word recognition is also a benchmark for growth in reading. Visually recognizing words and phrases is more efficient reading than auditorially decoding. As students develop fluency in reading they rely more on the visual recognition of words and phrases than continually sounding out individual words as they read. In fact, as readers progress they tend to vocalize less as they read. Word recognition also fosters comprehension of more complex words as skilled readers identify the roots embedded in multisyllabic constructions. For example, a reader skilled in recognizing roots will quickly decipher the meaning of "insightful" or "unsightly" or the phrase "short sightedness."

A key approach to this domain of foundational skills in reading is to teach to make connections. Just as with phonics, we teach to show the connection between specific sound-symbol relationships; with word recognition, we show connections between roots and affixes, word structures, and word families. These instructional connections are strengthened when ELLs see them as meaningful and contextualized.

Phonics and Word Recognition Activities

In this section, phonics and word recognition are provided according to performance level and grade level. I grouped the activities as follows: performance level 1 with grades K–1; performance level 2 with grades 2–3; and performance level 3 with grades 4–5. This is purely an organizational solution. The reality is that a 5th grade ELL at performance level 1 will need level 1-types of instructional support. Just because the ELL is a fifth grader, we cannot assume that she or he has acquired foundational level skills in English reading, so teachers treat the grade level groupings as conventional, but the performance level grouping as more fluid. It is entirely appropriate to apply performance level 1 activities to an older ELL if her or his proficiency level in English reading requires that support.

Foundational Reading Performance Levels

Foundational Reading Skills/ Performance Level Descriptors (PLDs)	Performance Level 1 Undeveloped foundational skills	Performance Level 2 Developing grade level foundational skills	Performance Level 3 Grade level foundational skills
Phonics and Word Recognition	Uses script other than English. Lacks basic one-to-one letter-sound correspondence. Scribbles or writes approximations of letters and simple words. Cannot write own name.	Produces the primary sound or many of the most frequent sounds for each vowel and consonant. Reads common, high-frequency words by sight.	Knows and applies grade-level phonics and word analysis skills in decoding words.

Kindergarten and 1st Grade

Activity for Performance Level 1 and Grades K–1: Uses script other than English; lacks basic one-to-one letter-sound correspondence; scribbles or writes approximations of letters and simple words; cannot write own name.

Common Core State Standards for Phonics and Word Recognition

CCSS.ELA-Literacy.RF.K.3 & RF.1.3
Know and apply grade-level phonics and word analysis skills in decoding words.
CCSS.ELA-Literacy.RF.K.3a
Demonstrate basic knowledge of one-to-one letter-sound correspondences by producing the primary sound or many of the most frequent sounds for each consonant.
CCSS.ELA-Literacy.RF.K.3b
Associate the long and short sounds with the common spellings (graphemes) for the five major vowels.

CCSS.ELA-Literacy.RF.K.3c

Read common high-frequency words by sight (e.g., the, of, to, you, she, my, is, are, do, does).

CCSS.ELA-Literacy.RF.K.3d

Distinguish between similarly spelled words by identifying the sounds of the letters that differ.

CCSS.ELA-Literacy.RF.1.3

Know and apply grade-level phonics and word analysis skills in decoding words.

CCSS.ELA-Literacy.RF.1.3a

Know the spelling-sound correspondences for common consonant digraphs.

CCSS.ELA-Literacy.RF.1.3b

Decode regularly spelled one-syllable words.

CCSS.ELA-Literacy.RF.1.3c

Know final-e and common vowel team conventions for representing long vowel sounds.

CCSS.ELA-Literacy.RF.1.3d

Use knowledge that every syllable must have a vowel sound to determine the number of syllables in a printed word.

CCSS.ELA-Literacy.RF.1.3e

Decode two-syllable words following basic patterns by breaking the words into syllables.

CCSS.ELA-Literacy.RF.1.3f

Read words with inflectional endings.

CCSS.ELA-Literacy.RF.1.3g

Recognize and read grade-appropriate irregularly spelled words.

Explore C-V-C Patterns. Initial phonics and word recognition involves discovering patterns. Using the following tables, students can take virtually any written text and search for words with similar C-V-C type patterns.

Table 6.1 is an example of how to explore letter patterns for simple words with 1–3 letters. Once students can recognize and distinguish vowels, they conduct searchers for different C-V-C type patterns in storybooks, textbooks, newspapers, and magazines. Students will find that not all patterns are represented in English.

Following is a table for exploring C-V-C patterns for words with 3–5 letters (Table 6.2). This table facilitates introducing vowel and consonant blends. It also introduces exploring words with a silent -e.

Table 6.1 Word Patterns With 1–3 Letters

V	V-C	C-V	C-V-C	V-C-C
A	Am	Be	Bat	Add
I	An	To	Bet	Ant
	As		Bow	Ask
	At		Car	Asp
	if		Cat	Ann
	I'm		Cow	
	In		Pat	
	Is		Put	
	It			
	On			

Table 6.2 Word Patterns With 3–6 Letters

V-V-C	C-V-V-C	C-V-C-C	C-C-V-C-C	C-V-C-e
Aim	Beat	Burn	Blind	BATe
Eon	Bean	Cart	Black	BONe
Ion	Beef	Putt	Climb	CARe
	Been		Stick	
	Beet			

Performance Level 1 ELLs oftentimes may not know how to write their name. I recommend that they practice writing their name with the tactile materials listed above. Table 6.3 invites them to find the C-V-C pattern for their own name.

Table 6.3 Finding a CVC Pattern

What is your CVC name pattern?	
Write your name.	PAUL
Write the CVC pattern for your name.	CVVC

Onsets and Rimes. The CCSS Appendix B recommends the manipulation of onsets and rimes with single syllable words. An onset is the consonant sound or sounds that may precede the vowel; rime is the vowel and all other consonant sounds that may follow the vowel.

Say the two parts slowly and then blend into a whole word:

◆ school onset /sch-/; rime /-ool/
◆ star onset /st-/; rime /-ar/
◆ place onset /pl-/; rime /-ace/
◆ all onset (none); rime /-all/

To enhance the meaning and increase the complexity of the task, apply the manipulation of onsets and rimes to familiar children's poetry. Ask students to identify the onset and rimes in "*H*ickory *d*ickory *d*ock/the mouse ran up the *cl*ock/the clock struck one/the mouse ran down . . ."

Note that there are multiple onsets and rimes and pairs of words that simply rhyme to a varying degree. Some are more obvious than others. As the teacher reads through the entire poem, compare the clear onsets-rimes pairs (hickory/dickory and dock/clock) from words that simply rhyme to various degrees (one/down). Which is a true onset and rime pair? Throughout the poem there are rhyming pairs that vary in whether they are true onset-rime combinations, particularly the words paired with the numbers on the clock (two/flew; three/fiddle-dee-dee; four/door; five/hive; and so forth).

Extend the activity by sorting words into true onset-rime pairs and word pairs that may just sound similar. Further extensions may include substituting words to see if true onset-rime pairs can be inserted, for example ". . . the clock struck three, the mouse _____ (had to flee or ran up a tree).

Activities for Performance Level 2 and Grades 2–3: Produces the primary sound or many of the most frequent sounds for each vowel and consonant; reads common, high-frequency words by sight.

Word Family Sorting and Categorizing. Sorting and categorizing are cognitively different activities. Sorting is placing items, in this case sorting words, into preset categories. Categorizing is more demanding because it asks the student to name the group or category for sorting. Students can sort or categorize groups of words into word families. The possibilities are endless. Take a look at the cover of this book. The cover illustration is a word-family-tree based on the consonant blend ST-.

Whereas past approaches to phonics and word recognition involved memorizing rules, these activities call for ELLs to apply habits of mind to learning to read. In the spirit of CCSS, the activities below call for students to explore and analyze components of the language, justify their thinking, and provide evidence or examples of their reasoning. Sorting is a skill required for categorizing, which is a skill required for rule building. I recommend beginning instruction with a preset sorting activity. Once the students are clear on the concept, move to a more open ended categorizing activity, which is followed below by rule building:

Examples of Preset Word Sorts:

- A, B, C . . . Sort by initial letter according to the alphabet.
- A, E, I, O, U, Y . . . Sort by initial vowel.
- Bl, Cl, Sl . . . Sort by similar consonant blends in initial position.
- -tt-,-ss-,-ll- . . . Sort by double consonants in medial position.
- -s,-ies,-ys . . . Sort by inflected endings with plural words.

Examples of Open-ended Categorizing Activities:

- Find at least 10 words with the letter S- at the beginning. Group them into families. Name the family group. (Possible families: Sa- words, Sl- words, St- words, Sch- words, and so forth.)
- Here is an interesting word, "**chocolate**," from the book, *Willy Wonka and the Chocolate Factory* by Roald Dahl (1964). Find other related words. Group them into families. Name how they are related. (Possible families: Ch- words; words with -co- in the middle; words ending in -ate; words ending with silent-e; three-syllable words; and so forth.)

Rule Building. Most commercial phonics programs deliver a set of rules for the various sound-symbol relationships in English. Rather than teaching a set of rules to students, it is much more engaging and meaningful to show ELLs a set of words and have them pose a possible rule and then test it out to see if it holds up in all or most other cases. Another aspect of this activity that I like about rule building is that it is virtually cost-free, unlike commercial programs.

Rule Building Employs Four Questions:

1. What is your rule?
2. When does it apply? (show examples)
3. Are there other examples that follow the rule, or not? (show exceptions or additional examples)
4. Is there a stronger rule?

- Provide a group of students with a collection of words that begin with "C."
- Ask them to sort the words into a hard-c /k-/ sound and a soft-c /s-/ sound (Table 6.4).

Table 6.4 Example of Word Sort

Word sort	
Hard-c /k-/	**Soft-c /s-/**
Candy	Cede
Cantaloupe	Cinnamon
Car	
Coat	
Cut	
Cuticle	

Ask the Four Questions:

Teacher: What is your rule?
Students: "Hard-c sounds happen when the C is followed by A, O, or U. Soft-c sounds happen when followed by E or I."
Teacher: When does it apply?
Students: Show their word sort and sound out each word.
Teacher: Are there other examples that follow the rule, or not? (Table 6.5)
Student #1: In Science I learned the word "cyclone."
Student #2: In Geography, I saw this word, "Cyprus."
Student #3: What about words like, "craft" and "climb"?

Table 6.5 Adding More
Vocabulary to the Word Sort

Word sort	
Hard-c /k-/	**Soft-c /s-/**
Candy	Cede
Cantaloupe	Cinnamon
Car	**Cyclone**
Coat	**Cyprus**
Cut	
Cuticle	
Craft	
Climb	

Teacher: Is there a stronger rule?

Students: Hard-c sounds happen when the C is followed by A, O, U, or a consonant. Soft-c sounds happen when followed by E, I, or Y.

Teacher: Are there other examples that follow the rule, or not?

Student #1:   What about words that begin with Ch-, like chocolate?

Student #2:   We need a new category to sort Ch- words.

Student #3:   What about the letter c in the middle of a word?

Reflection: This activity can go on into deeper understandings of how English functions. The teacher can assign more investigation and word sorting as homework, and then return to the rule building the following day. Once the students have exhausted a category and are satisfied with a rule, they would then be assigned to make a poster of their rule to be displayed for other students as a reference while reading. As a side note: this is an activity that uses both the auditory and visual sides of this domain at the same time. Cognitively, it is a more demanding type of activity because students are not only sorting, but they are reasoning, justifying their thinking, and establishing new categories.

Second and Third Grade

Common Core State Standards for Phonics and Word Recognition

CCSS.ELA-Literacy.RF.2.3 & RF.3.3
Know and apply grade-level phonics and word analysis skills in decoding words.

CCSS.ELA-Literacy.RF.2.3a
Distinguish long and short vowels when reading regularly spelled one-syllable words.
CCSS.ELA-Literacy.RF.2.3b
Know spelling-sound correspondences for additional common vowel teams.
CCSS.ELA-Literacy.RF.2.3c
Decode regularly spelled two-syllable words with long vowels.
CCSS.ELA-Literacy.RF.2.3d
Decode words with common prefixes and suffixes.
CCSS.ELA-Literacy.RF.2.3e
Identify words with inconsistent but common spelling-sound correspondences.
CCSS.ELA-Literacy.RF.2.3f
Recognize and read grade-appropriate irregularly spelled words.

CCSS.ELA-Literacy.RF.3.3a
Identify and know the meaning of the most common prefixes and derivational suffixes.
CCSS.ELA-Literacy.RF.3.3b
Decode words with common Latin suffixes.
CCSS.ELA-Literacy.RF.3.3c
Decode multi-syllable words.
CCSS.ELA-Literacy.RF.3.3d
Read grade-appropriate irregularly spelled words.

Activities for Performance Level 3 and Grades 4–5: Knows and applies grade-level phonics and word analysis skills in decoding words.

Fourth and Fifth Grade

Common Core State Standards for Phonics and Word Recognition

CCSS.ELA-Literacy.RF.4.3 & RF.5.3
Know and apply grade-level phonics and word analysis skills in decoding words.
CCSS.ELA-Literacy.RF.4.3a & RF.5.3a

Use combined knowledge of all letter-sound correspondences, syllabication patterns, and morphology (e.g., roots and affixes) to read accurately unfamiliar multisyllabic words in context and out of context.

Word-building Play. Building words is exploratory play that teaches prefixes, roots, and suffixes. It also shows that the language is malleable, like clay.

We manipulate the language to meet our needs. A famous example of how we naturally manipulate the language for our own needs is the recent introduction of the word "Selfie" into the lexicon. (Currently, my computer software highlights Selfie as a misspelling and offers the following alternative words: Elfie, Sulfide, Sulfite, Sheltie, or Sallie.) It wasn't long ago when the word "software" as opposed to "hardware" was coined.

There are numerous ways to build words, some more creative than others. Below are three examples of ways to conduct word-building activities: (1) Word building from a specific prefix, (2) Word building from a root word, and (3) Word building with noun adjuncts.

Word Building From a Prefix. Use one prefix with different root words to create a new word (Table 6.6). This is an easy starting point with word building. Students can simply look up words beginning with the same prefix to fill this table in. To increase the level of thinking, encourage students to make up a new word.

Table 6.6 Word Building From a Prefix

Prefix In-	Root	Constructed word
In-	action	Inaction
In-	articulate	Inarticulate
In-	comprehensible	Incomprehensible
In-	compatible	Incompatible
In-	separate	Inseparate (new)

Word Building From a Root Word. In this activity (Table 6.7), the root remains fixed while the student plays with prefixes and suffixes to build new words. In some cases, only the prefix, or only the suffix, is applied to build the word.

Table 6.7 Word Building From a Root Word

Prefix	Root -act-	Suffix	Constructed word
In-	-act-	-ion	Inaction
Un-	-act-	-ionable	Unactionable
Non-	-act-	-ive	Non-active
[no prefix]	-act-	-able	Actionable

Word Building Noun Adjuncts. *Adjunct* means to join together. In the case of noun adjuncts, first noun adds to the meaning of the second noun. It is the modifier of the second noun. Encourage students to use imaginative play to join two nouns in new and creative ways (Table 6.8). Funny adjuncts are welcome—imagine a banana with a built in zipper for peeling.

Table 6.8 Word Building Noun Adjuncts

Noun #1 (Modifier)	Noun #2	Adjunct
Traffic	Light	Traffic light
Bread	Basket	Bread basket
Banana	Zipper	Banana zipper
Jet	Cat	Jet cat

References

Dahl, R. (1964). *Willy Wonka and the Chocolate Factory*. New York: Alfred A. Knopf.

Moustafa, M. (2002). *Beyond traditional phonics: Research discoveries and reading instruction*. Portsmouth, NH: Heinemann.

National Institute of Child Health and Human Development (NICHD). (2000). Report of the National Reading Panel. Teaching children to read: An evidence-based assessment of the scientific research literature on reading and its implications for reading instruction: Reports of the subgroups (NIH Publication No. 00-4754). Washington, DC: U.S. Government Printing Office. www.nichd.nih.gov/ publications/nrp/report.htm

Shanahan, T. (2006). The National Reading Panel Report: Practical advice for teachers. www.learningpt.org/pdfs/literacy/nationalreading.pdf

7

Fluency
Kindergarten–Grade 5

English Language Learners and Fluency

As stated in Chapter 3, fluency, as defined by the National Reading Panel (2000) and Samuels (2006), is comprised of three components: accuracy, automaticity, and prosody. For ease of use, I will sometimes interchange terminology for automaticity (rate or pacing) and prosody (expression).

- ◆ Accuracy: decoding by correctly generating phonological representations of each word, either because it is part of the reader's sight-word vocabulary or by use of a more effortful decoding strategy such as sounding out the word.
- ◆ Automaticity: quickly recognizing words with little cognitive effort or attention.
- ◆ Prosody: reading with proper phrasing and expression.

Fluency became a significant component of early literacy in the 1970s with the work of LaBerge and Samuels (1974), who posited that students who read text fluently, versus reading with exclusive attention to decoding, would attend more to the meaning of the text. Their work concentrated on the cognitive processing theory of automaticity, which essentially stated that as we develop automaticity our brains are then able to attend to other cognitive processes. Consequently, greater levels of fluency were correlated with increased comprehension in reading. This notion of fluency has been supported by the research literature (Kuhn & Stahl, 2003; NRP, 2000; Perfetti, Goldman, & Hogaboam, 1979; and Rasinski, 2004).

Very few empirical research studies, however, inform the practice of fluency instruction with English language learners. For example, the National Literacy Panel Report (August & Shanahan, 2006) only identified two studies on fluency instruction with ELLs (and De la Colina, Parker, Hasbrouuck, & Lara-Alecio, 2001; Wexler, Vaughn, Roberts, & Denton, 2010). Even with this small evidence base, the results appear to be consistent with English-only fluency research.

Generally, fluency development is fostered by repeated reading activities; however, Wexler et al. (2010) and De la Colina et al. (2001) brought to light several findings with reading fluency that are unique to ELLs. First of all, fluency increases as ELLs read culturally relevant texts. Additionally, there is a correlation between reading fluently in English and fluent reading in the primary language (L1). Along similar lines, ELLs with limited proficiency read more fluently in their dominant language (L1 or L2). These findings have important implications for the classroom teacher with regard to text selection and language usage.

Rasinski (1990) contributed another research finding that I believe holds true for ELLs, even though the study was conducted with English-only students. He found a close relationship between fluency and reading-while-listening to quality models of reading aloud. This finding applies to reading-while-listening to a teacher reading aloud, and it also applies to using media to foster fluency, such as reading while listening to audiobooks in MP3 formats. Quality modeling of reading demonstrates the three components of fluency noted above, namely accuracy, automaticity, and prosody for the listener.

Three Ways to Develop Fluency With ELLs: Culturally Relevant Text Selection, Primary Language Use, and Modeling

Based upon the above-cited research of reading fluency, in addition to conventional practices of repeated reading, classroom teachers of ELLs should pay particular attention to selecting culturally relevant texts, invite students to read in both English and their primary language (L_1 and L_2), and provide quality models of reading through reading aloud and the use of recorded media.

Culturally Relevant Texts. Although school districts take primary responsibility for providing reading materials to classrooms, selecting text sets for reading has been ceded back to classroom teachers with the advent of the

CCSS. It is incumbent upon the classroom teach to select engaging and relevant texts for ELLs to foster increased fluency and comprehension.

Teachers responding to the recommendations of the CCSS will select a wide array of texts including seminal works, related material that reflects other cultural perspectives, informational texts from both English speaking countries and countries of origin of immigrant students. Sometimes, locally relevant texts such as articles from community news sources may be appropriate. The many free sources available via the Internet will require a discerning eye, but more culturally appropriate material is available than ever.

Primary Language Use. Before beginning this discussion, I'd like to emphasize that the goal of regular classroom instruction is to develop proficiency in English. Yet, the cognitive process of fluency is language neutral to high degree. In other words, reading is reading, no matter which language. Nevertheless, there persists a common fallacy that claims that ELLs should use only English in the classroom for learning. You may have overheard a novice teacher yell at an ELL, "Speak English!" However, when primary language support is strategically applied, it is one of the best tools to help ELLs. I know that it seems counter-intuitive to use another language to develop English proficiency; but inviting strategic use of primary language support is invaluable to developing English proficiency. Languages don't compete with each other in the brain; they in fact, help each other understand words and grammatical structures. As stated above, inviting students to read in their home languages can enhance reading fluency in English.

Consider this teaching scenario: The primary reading text is *Frog and Toad Are Friends* by Arnold Lobel (1970). Putting together a text set, the classroom teacher would include informational texts about the differences between frogs and toads. Articles on the differences abound in English and in other languages. Inviting the ELLs to read about those differences in their primary language will have multiple benefits to developing English. First of all, the students get more opportunities to read texts about the same topic. Secondly, they increase their comprehension of the story by reading about the differences in their own language. Thirdly, as students read in English and their primary language, they may identify cognates, or key terms shared across languages, such as **reptile** in English and *reptil* in Spanish. Finally, the ELLs' families can now participate in their learning in a more meaningful way because they can help their children read in their own language.

Modeling Reading, Reciting, Singing, and Media. As mentioned earlier, **automaticity** is developed by repeated reading; but notions of **prosody** are developed by listening to models demonstrating phrasing and tone. Reading-while-listening (Rasinski, 1990) is the important component here.

The students have the same text in hand that the teacher is reading aloud. And they follow along as the teacher reads. They are encouraged to point out words and vocalize along as they read. This emphasizes the importance of having multiple sets of books on hand. Teachers spend hundreds of dollars of their own money to equip classrooms with book sets. With the advent of the Common Core, let's hope that school districts will reinvest in quality fiction and non-fiction texts for all students.

How the teacher reads a book with students can greatly increase the benefits of the reading-while-listening experience. Reading with expression increases the level of attention the ELLs will give, and it establishes the model for how you'd like the students to read. Additionally, changing voices to match the story characters' words will increase the ELLs' comprehension and interest. Further, pointing out key words and key components of the illustrations will enhance the meaning of the reading experience. Finally, reading at a slightly slower pace with attention to clear pronunciation of words will also help the ELL hear how to pronounce and read words accurately. Using books with multiple and vivid illustrations for reading-while-listening is essential to support ELLs. If the students get lost in the words, quality illustrations guide the listener/reader to the meaning of the text.

All of the above applies to reciting poems and singing songs. Reciting poems and singing songs from colorful and illustrated charts on display around the room is not only a delightful way to develop fluency; but it is downright sneaky. I say "sneaky" because it doesn't feel like formal learning when we chant and sing; but the same processes are in place. Once students learn a poem or a song, it is repeated over and over. Students chant on the playground, sing in line for lunch, and at times when their minds stray from the lesson at hand, they look up at charts on display and quietly read the words to their favorite poems and songs. Poems and songs bring an enhanced performance aspect to reading that requires all the components of fluency (accuracy, automaticity, and prosody), plus rhythm and melody. With poems and songs, we don't call it repeated reading, we call it rehearsal; and the students perform those poems and songs for each other, their families, and the community. Think of the level of language development when children sing, "Doe, a deer, a female deer/ray a drop of golden sun . . ." (Rogers & Hammerstein, 1959).

The final aspect of modeling for fluency that needs attention here is using media. There is a wealth of free material available to teachers that should be utilized and assigned to students to use for reading practice at home. Currently any required text is available in an audio format. There are hundreds of audiobooks available at no cost on YouTube, via the public library, and Internet sites such as www.openculture.com/freeaudiobooks and https://librivox.org/.

The selection is extensive in English and many other languages, so that students can read while listening at home. Another approach is to utilize the text-to-voice feature on many e-Readers. Text-to-voice applications probably work better with informational texts than literary texts because informational texts don't require the need for multiple voices to match the characters of the story. Although the voice sounds somewhat robotic, and pronunciation is suspect at times, e-Readers can help make a text more comprehensible, too.

Activities for Fluency

Foundational Reading Performance Levels for Fluency

As stated in Chapter 1, performance level descriptors (PLDs) provide a quick reference for discerning at what level of fluency the ELL is functioning. The PLDs are not comprehensive, but illustrative of key reading behaviors at the foundational skills level.

Performance Levels for Fluency

Foundational Reading Skills/ Performance Level Descriptors (PLDs)	**Performance Level 1** Undeveloped foundational skills	**Performance Level 2** Developing grade level foundational skills	**Performance Level 3** Grade level foundational skills
Fluency	Unable to decode simple words in a sentence in English.	Reads simple text with some accuracy, pacing, and expression. Self-corrects some errors.	Reads with sufficient accuracy and fluency to support comprehension. Self-corrects errors.

Common Core Foundational Skills Standards for Fluency, K–5

There is quite a bit of overlap with the Common Core K–5 Fluency Standards. In order to have an easier grasp the fluency standards, I've grouped and condensed them to reduce repetition. The groups are as follows: Purpose and Understanding, Accuracy and Prosody, and Contextual Support and Self-Correction. Each standard is referenced according to its grade level.

Grades K–5

Common Core State Standards for Fluency

> *CCSS Anchor Standard for Fluency: K–5*
> *Read with sufficient accuracy and fluency to support comprehension.*

Purpose and Understanding: K–5

CCSS.ELA-LITERACY.RF.K.4

Read emergent-reader texts with purpose and understanding.

CCSS.ELA-LITERACY.RF.1.4., 2.4., 3.4., 4.4., 5.4.A

Read grade-level text with purpose and understanding.

Accuracy and Prosody: Grades 1–5

CCSS.ELA-LITERACY.RF.1.4., and 2.4.B

Read grade-level text orally with accuracy, appropriate rate, and expression on successive readings.

CCSS.ELA-LITERACY.RF.3.4., 4.4., 5.4.B

Read grade-level prose and poetry orally with accuracy, appropriate rate, and expression on successive readings.

Contextual Support and Self-Correction: Grades 1–5

CCSS.ELA-LITERACY.RF.5.4., 4.4, 3.4, 2.4., 1.4.C

Use context to confirm or self-correct word recognition and understanding, re-reading as necessary.

Activity for Performance Level 1 ELLs: Unable to Decode Simple Words in a Sentence

Adapt Familiar Songs. Rasinski and Padak (2011) and others recommend using songs and poetry to develop fluency in early reading. Sing simple songs that are easy to illustrate, act out and include repetition. Go to a public domain sight such as The Public Domain Info Project (www.pdinfo.com/Public-Domain-Music-List.php) to find lists of children's music.

In order to enhance the English language development experience, take the familiar song and change the words to extend the language. This increases the richness of meaning and complexity of the language experience. For example, I took the popular children's song "The Bear Went Over the Mountain" and inserted groups of words that shared the same meaning in each stanza.

Adaptation of "The Bear Went Over the Mountain" by Paul Boyd-Batstone

(Sing to the tune of "For He's a Jolly Good Fellow")

The bear **looked** over the mountain,   The bear **admired** the mountain,
The bear **considered** the mountain,   I hope he doesn't **see** me.

I hope he doesn't see me
I hope he doesn't see me.

The bear **ran up to** the mountain,
The bear **came up to** the mountain,
The bear **arrived at** the mountain,
I hope he isn't **near me**.

I hope he isn't near me.
I hope he isn't near me.

The bear **inspected** the mountain,
The bear **searched** all through the mountain,
The bear **examined** the mountain,
I hope he doesn't **find** me.

I hope he doesn't see me.
I hope he isn't near me.
The bear looked over the mountain,
The bear ran up to the mountain,
The bear inspected the mountain,
I hope he doesn't find me.

Meaning and complexity complement each other. Complex or multi-syllabic words are not difficult for ELLs to learn if they are meaningful. For example, I've observed ELLs who struggle with a simple word like "the," but have no trouble learning a word like "valentine." The words that I grouped for the English adaptation (looked, considered, admired, see) are both simple and complex. Their grouping provides meaningful context. The complex words are surrounded by simpler words with similar meaning. As they sing the song, the ELLs are increasing fluency, meaning, and complexity of language.

I also translated the above adaptation into Spanish to tap into the primary language (L_1). Providing primary language support involves families in the singing and fluency experience with their children. Send both versions (English and Spanish) of the song home to sing as homework. To be honest, the Spanish version does not use the same level of language complexity as the English adaptation above. However, it gives families the opportunity to sing along with their child and sets up the opportunity for the ELL to sing in two languages at home.

El Oso Mira al Cerro
Traducido por Paul Boyd-Batstone

El oso mira al cerro,
El oso mira al cerro,
El oso mira al cerro,
A ver si me vió.

A ver si me vió.
A ver si me vió.

Llega hasta el cerro,
Llega hasta el cerro,
Llega hasta el cerro,
A ver si me oló.

A ver si me oló.
A ver si me oló.

Camina sobre el cerro,
Camina sobre el cerro,
Camina sobre el cerro,
Y no me encontró.

A ver si me vió.
A ver si me oló,
El oso mira al cerro,
Llega hasta el cerro,
Camina sobre el cerro,
Y no me encontró.

(Lyrics in Spanish by Paul
Boyd-Batstone)

Give the students the opportunity to rehearse the song in small groups or pairs. To increase the meaning of the adapted song in English, ask the students to role play the scenario of the bear looking, approaching, and searching for one or more of the students on the mountain. Use a simple prop such as projecting a picture of a mountain on screen as a backdrop for the action. Ask the students to create simple costumes to represent the bear and children hiking the mountain.

Next to the written text of each stanza of the song, have the students draw illustrations of each scenario as the bear gets closer and closer. Select pairs of children to illustrate each stanza of the song in a larger format on poster sized piece of chart paper. As you sing in a group refer to the poster-sized charted song. Ask students to point to the key words.

Activity for Level 2 ELLs: Reads Simple Text With Some Accuracy, Pacing, and Expression, and Self-Corrects Some Errors

Memorize and Recite Poetry. In order to develop reading accuracy, pacing, and expression, students can memorize and recite poetry. Pacing and expression, in particular, are performance-based tasks. The students need to rehearse and then perform for their peers. In this case, I've selected the text of "Twinkle, Twinkle Little Star" (text of the poem provided by Burt, 2005). We know the tune and the first stanza, but note the richness of the language in the following stanzas.

Twinkle, Twinkle, Little Star

(Anonymous)

Twinkle, twinkle, little star!
How I wonder what you are,
Up above the world so high,
Like a diamond in the sky.

When the glorious sun is set,
When the grass with dew is wet,
Then you show your little light,
Twinkle, twinkle all the night.

In the dark-blue sky you keep,
And often through my curtains peep,
For you never shut your eye,
Till the sun is in the sky.

As your bright and tiny spark
Guides the traveler in the dark,
Though I know not what you are,
Twinkle, twinkle, little star!

Provide initial vocabulary instruction. Preparing for reading fluency begins with vocabulary development. Select key vocabulary from each stanza of the poem. Note that some words need to be taught as a phrase to grasp the meaning in the text. For example:

- First Stanza: Twinkle, wonder, world, diamond
- Second Stanza: glorious, sun is set, dew
- Third Stanza: dark-blue sky, curtains, peep
- Fourth Stanza: tiny spark, guides, traveler

Divide the class into four groups according to the four stanzas of the poem. Within each stanza-group assign key vocabulary to pairs of students with the following directions:

- Make a poster about your assigned vocabulary word or phrase.
- Include in the poster the following:
  1. The vocabulary word, or phrase, at the top written in big bold lettering
  2. The definition of the word or phrase.
  3. Copy the stanza from the poem where the word or phrase occurs.
  4. Draw and caption illustrations of what the word is like.
  5. Find and list another word that sounds like key word.
     - Post each poster on the walls around the room, arranged by stanza-group.
     - Present your poster to the entire class.

Now that the vocabulary is addressed, students can begin to rehearse reading for accuracy, pacing, and expression.

Accuracy: Encourage students to refer to the posters on the walls of the room as they read each stanza of the poem for accuracy. Help individual students who struggle with specific words.

Pacing: Identify points in the poem to pause and breathe. Specify shorter pauses marked by the commas and longer pauses between stanzas marked with a period. Note the cadence of the poem with seven beats per line of poetry. The first six beats are paired (1. . .2, 3. . .4, 5. . .6), and the final, seventh beat is longer and is followed by a pause.

Twinkle/twinkle/ little/ *star*. . .

1. . .2 / 3. . .4 / 5. . .6/ *7* (short pause)

Use hand motions to indicate the beat pairs and the long seventh beat and pause. Hold hands up with palms facing out. Move the hands back and forth with a twist of the wrist to indicate the paired beats. Spread the fingers open and pause at the seventh beat. This applies to every line of the poem. For enhanced meaning, ask the students to develop more meaningful gestures to represent the cadence and the meaning of key words, particularly those at the ends of the lines and stanzas.

To add nuance to the pacing, once students have mastered the seven beats of the poem, ask them to vary the speed of the lines of poetry so they don't sound quite so robotic. Practice reading some lines slowly and others at a quicker pace. See which lines sound more natural when the pace is slowed or quickened.

Expression: All students, and ELLs in particular, need modeling to develop skill in reading with expression. The teacher is the primary model for expression in reading. Consider pitch and volume as you model expression. As a model, the teacher should read with a slight exaggeration in expression. Read a stanza of the poem with expression, and then have the students read the same stanza trying to mirror how you—the teacher—read the stanza.

Have some fun with expression. Write different character roles on flash cards, such as Pirate, Super Hero, Little Old Lady, Timid Child, Corporate CEO, Opera Singer, a Favorite Cartoon Character, and U.S. Politician. Help the students imagine how each of the characters would sound as they read aloud. Consider facial expressions and body position as they read. Then model, for example, how a pirate might read the poem in a gravelly voice, out of the side of the mouth: "Twinkle, twinkle little star . . . Yaaarrrr!"

Role-Play Read Around

1. Divide the class into groups according to the stanzas of the poem. (Four stanzas-four groups).
2. Arrange each small group into their own circles, facing each other. (Four circle groups around the room.)
3. Supply each group with a stanza of the poem in large print so that all can see the stanza from where they are sitting.
4. Place the role-play cards in a bag or basket for each stanza-group.
5. Each student selects a role-play card.
6. In turn, each student reads the stanza aloud individually to the rest of the group. (With some ELLs, consider pairing students to build confidence.)
7. The first student reader in each group picks a role-play card then reads to the group "in character," doing the best imitation of that character that they can.
8. The next student follows by selecting another role-play card.
9. Finish by having each stanza group select an individual or pair of students to read their stanza aloud to the entire class.
10. Have the selected students stand in front of the class and read the entire poem with the different characters representing each stanza.
11. Have fun. Encourage laughter and over-the-top expressiveness.

Recitation for an Audience: Now that vocabulary, accuracy, pacing, and expression have been developed, it is time for the performance. Require that students memorize the poem to recite for an audience.

It is cumbersome to have every student recite the same poem in front of the entire class. After the third or fourth recitation, you may lose the attention of the class. To address this problem, incentivize the reading performance: you must earn the opportunity to recite the poem from memory before the class.

Return the students to their stanza-groups. Provide small group time in class to work on memorizing the entire poem. Assign homework to memorize and recite the poem. (To ensure that the students are working on memorizing the poem at home, require that the parent or guardian sign off that the student recited the poem from memory at home.)

In the small stanza-groups, students will take turns reciting the poem for their peers. Then the group confers to select one of their members to recite the poem for the entire class.

Finish off the activity with the four selected students reciting the entire poem for the whole class. Teachers should be alert to making the whole class performance a celebratory time, recognizing how vulnerable a student may feel in front of peers.

Provide rules for audience behavior, such as: listen to each recitation with full attention, applaud and encourage at the end of the recitation, and offer affirmations ("very accurate recitation," "nice pacing," "great expression"). Teachers can enhance the atmosphere of the recitation by dimming the lights and playing appropriate background music as the student recites the poem.

Activity for Level 3 ELLs: Reads With Sufficient Accuracy and Fluency to Support Comprehension and Self-Corrects Errors

Reading Historic Speeches. Using historical speeches to develop fluency employs cross-curricular interconnections and increased text complexity. Although the CCSS does not provide content-specific standards for History-Social Science, a typical 5th grade content standard from the Revolutionary War Period reads as follows:

> Describe the views, lives, and impact of key individuals during this period (e.g., King George III, Patrick Henry, Thomas Jefferson, George Washington, Benjamin Franklin, John Adams). (California History-Social Science Standards, 2009, p. 18)

To demonstrate how to develop fluency and teach History, I selected the famous "Give me liberty or give me death" speech by Patrick Henry. The following in the final paragraph of the text:

> "It is in vain, sir, to extenuate the matter. Gentlemen may cry, Peace, Peace—but there is no peace. The war is actually begun! The next gale that sweeps from the north will bring to our ears the clash of resounding arms! Our brethren are already in the field! Why stand we here idle? What is it that gentlemen wish? What would they have? Is life so dear, or peace so sweet, as to be purchased at the price of chains and slavery? Forbid it, Almighty God! I know not what course others may take; but as for me, give me liberty or give me death!" (Patrick Henry, 1775)

Provide Historical Context. Providing historical context is crucial to understanding the meaning and power of Patrick Henry's speech. Since it is somewhat pushing the scope of this book to demonstrate how to teach history, I will leave that to the history experts. However, teaching the historical context would explore the root causes of the American Revolutionary War including the following topics and themes:

1. The political, religious, and economic ideas and interests that brought about the Revolution, including resistance to British rule, the Stamp Act, the Townshend Acts, Coercive Acts, and so forth).

2. The makeup and actions of the first and second Continental Congresses.
3. The people and events surrounding the drafting and signing of the Declaration of Independence.

Listen and Practice With Digital Media. There are multiple digital sources that capture this historic speech, for example:

◆ Colonial Williamsburg at www.history.org/almanack/life/politics/giveme.cfm
◆ Yale Law School's The Avalon Project at http://avalon.law.yale.edu/18th_century/patrick.asp
◆ YouTube videos: http://youtube/Cjwonvar-3g

All of the above are excellent resources, but for the purposes of developing fluency, I recommend that students view the YouTube video that I referenced because it provides the text for students to read along with a professional reader. Students can use the videos to help them develop accuracy, pacing, and expression as they read along in class with headphones, at a local library, or as homework from their home computers.

Digital Presentation of the Speech. Consuming digital media is just one aspect of using technological tools in learning. The other aspect of the instruction is to equip students to use the tools of technology to produce media. Utilizing digital tools is in alignment with Listening-Speaking Standards from the Common Core:

> CCSS.ELA-LITERACY.SL.5.5
> Include multimedia components (e.g., graphics, sound) and visual displays in presentations when appropriate to enhance the development of main ideas or themes.

This is another example of the interconnectedness of the CCSS. Employing graphics, sounds, visual displays (photos, video clips, clip art, and diagrams) in presentations cultivate meaningful learning experiences for all students. ELLs will develop fluency with the speech as the work to produce a multimedia presentation of a portion of Patrick Henry's speech.

A very intuitive and educator-friendly venue for developing a multimedia presentation is Prezi.com. I recommend the platform because it includes all the essential presentation software tools needed to create a digital project. There are also hundreds of public Prezis that can be viewed as models for your students. One such public presentation about Patrick Henry is found at http://prezi.com/u4bstit8dw-l/patrick-henryjourny-to-freedom/.

With any digital project, I recommend that you start simply. Below is a very simple template adapted from the final paragraph of Patrick Henry's speech. The sample template is divided into five slides or components. The first slide is simply a title page, the following four slides drawn from excerpts of the speech.

Directions

1. Use the sample template below to create a multimedia presentation of Patrick Henry's speech.
2. Include a wide range of visuals including clip art, photos, diagrams and video clips.
3. Add sound effects and background music.
4. Narrate the speech with a recording of your own reading, or shared reading. (No audio recordings of other people reading will be allowed.)
5. You may adapt the template to fit your presentation structure and content; but you must, at least, include the provided excerpt of the speech in its entirety.

Slide #1

Title Slide: Patrick Henry's "Give me liberty or give me death!" speech, 1775
By [Insert student(s) name(s)]
Grade:
School:

Slide #2

It is in vain, sir, to extenuate the matter. Gentlemen may cry, Peace, Peace—but there is no peace. The war is actually begun!

Slide #3

The next gale that sweeps from the north will bring to our ears the clash of resounding arms! Our brethren are already in the field!

Slide #4

Why stand we here idle? What is it that gentlemen wish? What would they have?

Slide #5

> Is life so dear, or peace so sweet, as to be purchased at the price of chains and slavery? Forbid it, Almighty God!

Slide #6

> I know not what course others may take; but as for me, give me liberty or give me death!

When the media presentations are done, have students share their presentations for the entire class. Rather than doing presentations in a linear fashion, I recommend that you set up a number of computers in the classroom or in a computer lab. Have the presentations set up on auto-play mode with a repeating loop so that peers can walk from computer station to station viewing other students' productions. Finish with a class discussion about the quality of the reading and the production. Save the best presentation for the next class to see and improve upon.

Competitive Performance. For this final idea, I'd like to give credit to my good friends at Patrick Henry Elementary School, Long Beach Unified School District in California. This award winning, dual immersion (Spanish/English) bilingual school conducts a Patrick Henry speech competition every year among the 4th and 5th grade students. The winner of the school-wide competition gets to dress up as Patrick Henry and give the speech to the entire educational community at their awards ceremony near the end of the school year.

The Patrick Henry speech competition begins with students receiving a text of the speech. They participate in a wide range of learning activities that give meaningful context to the text of the speech. Vocabulary instruction is conducted in class. There is also time provided for rehearsing the speech in pairs and small groups.

At a designated date, each classroom listens to volunteers read the speech. They are evaluated using a Fluency Rubric like the one provided below. The 4–6 students from each classroom are sent to a special assembly in the school auditorium for competitive tryouts for the opportunity to speak in front of the whole educational community. Although each participant receives a certificate for upholding the voice of Patrick Henry, only one student is selected with one alternate reader. One would think that English Only speaking students would be at an advantage in this competition; however, in recent years at Patrick Henry Elementary School, ELLs have won the competition an equal number of times as English Only speakers.

Formative Assessment Rubric. The following rubric (Table 7.1) can be used by the teacher to evaluate the reading fluency of any student and it can also be used by students for peer assessment and feedback.

The rubric includes three criteria on a four-point scale. The criteria are Accuracy, Rate, and Expression. At the base of each numeric column is a place to subtotal the points. On the far right of the rubric, is column for writing brief comments and for totaling an overall score from the three criteria. The maximum number of points the rubric generates is 12 = 3 (criteria) × 4 (points). As the evaluator listens for reading fluency, they need only place a check in the box that most closely describes the reading behavior. Summing each column and then totaling the bottom row scores provides a number for recording and comparing growth.

Students may apply this rubric to their own reading by listening to a recording of their own voice reading a selected text. Peers can use this rubric to assess each other's reading fluency. Teachers can also use this rubric to explain to parents the areas of strengths and needs evident in a student's fluency.

Table 7.1 Fluency Rubric

Fluency	4	3	2	1	Comments
Accuracy	Accurate pronunciation (No errors)	Some words mispronounced (1–4 errors)	Most words mispronounced (5 or more errors)	Multiple errors (10 or more)	
Rate	Proper pacing and pauses	Hesitates to decipher some words	Frequent hesitation to decode most words	Struggles to decode each word	
Expression	Fully expressive voice	Some expression in voice	Little expression in voice	No expression used	
Points (Sum each column)					**Total Points** (Sum the row. Max 12 points)

References

August, D. & Shanahan, T. (2006). *Developing literacy in second language learners: Report of the National Literacy Panel on language minority children and youth.* Mahwah, NJ: Lawrence Erlbaum Associate Publishers.

Burt, M. E. (Ed.) (2005). "Twinkle, twinkle little star." (Anonymous). The Project Gutenberg e-book of poems every child should know. Retrieved August 30, 2014 from www.gutenberg.org/ebooks/16436

California Department of Education (2009). *History-social science standards for California public schools*, Grade 5, p. 18.

De la Colina, D., Guadalupe, M., Parker, R. I., Hasbrouck, J. E., & Lara-Alecio, R. (2001). Intensive intervention in reading fluency for at-risk beginning Spanish readers. *Bilingual Research Journal*, 25(4), 503–538.

Henry, P. (1775). "Give me liberty or give me death." Speech he made to the Virginia Convention in 1775, at St. John's Church in Richmond, Virginia. http://en.wikipedia.org/wiki/Give_me_liberty,_or_give_me_death!

Kuhn, M. R., & Stahl, S. A. (2003). Fluency: A review of developmental and remedial practices. *Journal of educational psychology*, 95(1), 3.

LeBerge, D. & Samuels, S. J. (1974). Toward a theory of automatic information processing in reading. *Cognitive Psychology*, 6(2), 293–323.

Lobel, A. (1970). *Frog and Toad are friends.* New York: Harper Collins.

National Reading Panel (US), National Institute of Child Health, & Human Development (US). (2000). *Report of the national reading panel: Teaching children to read: An evidence-based assessment of the scientific research literature on reading and its implications for reading instruction: Reports of the subgroups.* National Institute of Child Health and Human Development, National Institutes of Health.

Perfetti, C. A., Goldman, S. R., & Hogaboam, T. W. (1979). Reading skill and the identification of words in discourse context. *Memory & Cognition*, 7(4), 273–282.

Rasinski, T. V. (1990). Effects of repeated reading and listening-while-reading on reading fluency. *Journal of Educational Research*, 83, 147–150.

Rasinski, T. (March, 2004). What research says about reading: Creating fluent readers. ASCD, *Educational Leadership*, 61(6), 46–51. www.ascd.org/publications/educational-leadership/mar04/vol61/num06/Creating-Fluent-Readers.aspx

Rasinski, T., & Padak, N. (Eds.). (2011). From fluency to comprehension: Powerful instruction through authentic reading. New York: Guilford Publications.

Rogers, R. & Hammerstein, O. (1959). Do-Re-Mi. *The Sound of Music.*

Samuels, S. J. (2006). Toward a model of reading fluency. In S.J. Samuels & A.E. Farstrup, Eds., *What research has to say about fluency instruction*, pp. 24–46. Newark, DE: International Reading Association.

Wexler, J., Vaughn, S., Roberts, G., & Denton, C. A. (2010). The efficacy of repeated reading and wide reading practice for high school students with severe reading disabilities. *Learning Disabilities Research & Practice*, 25(1), 2–10.

8

Lesson Planning for ELLs
Common Core/Differentiated Instruction/Assessment

The Lesson Plan as a Tool for Differentiated Instruction

There are a number of models and critiques about lesson design (John, 2006). Some teachers and school administrators would like to see just one lesson plan format for all instruction. I understand the impetus for one-size fits all in lesson planning, but I see the lesson plan as a specific tool for a unique purpose and population. For example Grant and Sleeter (2006) provided a model for lesson design to emphasize multicultural education; Courey, et al. (2013) offered a Universal Design for Learning (UDL) model to address special needs students; and science educators have found the Five E Lesson Plan beneficial for the inductive and exploratory nature of science (Goldston, et al., 2010). Each is a specific tool to meet the requirements of a subject area and the student population.

The focus of this chapter is to offer a lesson plan template for ELLs that encompasses Common Core aligned instruction, differentiated learning activities and learning outcomes by language level, and formative assessment in alignment with CCSS and the differentiated student outcomes. The value of using a differentiated lesson plan is that in a single lesson plan the needs of all students are addressed, ELL and English-only students alike.

Writing Lesson Plans Like a Cookbook

The metaphor that I like to use for lesson planning is a recipe from a cookbook. When you read a quality cookbook each recipe provides essential information that guides the chef to creating a final product. There will be some background information about the food to be cooked, the occasion that is appropriate for the dish, the materials needed. There will be step-by-step procedures aligned with the initial information that includes how to prepare the food. There will oftentimes be alternative ways to prepare or present the food. And it will include a description of the final product. The authentic assessment piece is "The proof of the pudding is in the eating." (Cervantes, 1604/2003).

Another aspect of cookbooks that informs how to write a lesson plan is the discourse style employed. Cookbooks are written in a verb-driven, directive style. The chef, as the subject, is implied or understood. Cookbooks begin directives with a verb in command form, such as "measure three cups of flower" or "stir for five minutes" or "serve over rice." You would find it comical to read a cookbook that was written with "the chef" inserted in every sentence, such as "the chef will measure . . ." "the chef will stir . . ." or "the chef will serve. . . ." Yet, as a teacher educator, I am amazed at the number of lesson plans that insert, "The teacher will . . ." at the beginning of every sentence. My recommendation is to follow the discourse style of a cookbook and begin directives with an active verb in command form, we know that the plan is written to the instructor. Please see Table 8.1 in which I provide a categorized list of verbs to be used in literacy instruction. Select a verb from the list to begin sentences in the Step-by-Step section of the lesson plan format.

When writing a lesson plan, follow the discourse style of a cookbook:

◆ Write clear directives with an active verb in command form
◆ Provide alternatives
◆ Describe the outcome

Experienced lesson planners will tell you that they do not write plans in a linear fashion, from top to bottom. More likely, the lesson planning process utilizes a backwards design model (McTighe & Thomas, 2005). In short, you begin planning by establishing a clear outcome for the students first; then work back to map out the pathway including assessments in alignment with the appropriate content standards, strategies/activities, and materials.

The true test of a quality lesson plan is to see if someone else can use it to teach your lesson with clarity and confidence. Write lesson plans as if you

Table 8.1 Instructionally Related Verbs in Command Form to Use When Writing Lesson Plans

Strategies	Listening	Writing	Reading	Speaking
Arrange	Analyze	Capitalize	Blend	Ask
Choose	Ask	Craft	Decode	Conclude
Clarify	Clarify	Create	Follows word	Confirm
Compare	Determine	Define	Highlight	Deliver
Contrast	Discern	Describe	Re-read	Describe
Confirm	Distinguish	Edit	Read	Indicate
Connect (ideas)	Follow	Illustrate	Study	Justify
Demonstrate	Direct	Indent	Track	Quote
Generate	Recognize	Organize	Use references	Recite
Classify	Gesture	Outline	Find meaning	Recount
Match	Identify	Print	Decipher	Relate
Plan	Point out, to	Revise	Interpret	Report
Present	Question	Rework	Infer	Represent
Provide	React	Spell		Request
Select	Recognize	Summarize		Re-tell
Support	Respond	Write		Share (information)
Use (strategies)				State
Organize				

(Adapted from Boyd-Batstone, P. (2007). *Anecdotal records assessment: An Observational Tool With a Standards-Based Focus*. Norwood, MA: Christopher Gordon Publishers.)

Use **backwards design** to plan a lesson:

1. Start by defining clear outcomes from your lesson.
2. Align the outcomes with the appropriate Common Core standard(s).
3. Differentiate the outcome according to language levels.
4. Articulate the academic goals for the lesson.
5. Identify or create the formative assessment(s) to measure each outcome.
6. Identify or develop strategies and student activities to reach the outcomes.
7. Select the materials and resources needed to reach the outcomes.

were writing the plan for someone else to teach. This helps ensure a number of important factors. First, it ensures that the plan is complete, without gaps or missing details. Secondly, it clarifies the plan because it is written in language designed to communicate, rather than using cryptic notes, which only the author of the plan understands.

> Write lesson plans as if you were writing the plan for someone else to teach to ensure:
>
> ◆ Completeness: No gaps or missing details.
> ◆ Clarity: Written to communicate, without cryptic notations only understood by the author.

Sections of a Differentiated Lesson Plan in a Common Core Context

There are three sections to the lesson plan, designed to provide the essential information and organization for planning a complete lesson. They are Preliminary Information, Lesson Procedures and Differentiation, and Outcomes and Assessment (Table 8.2).

A. *Preliminary Information* includes the essential information to situate the instruction and identify materials and resources. This section answers the questions, for the instructor and the administrator, about who is being taught, the level of instruction, and the subject area. It references appropriate Common Core standards and establishes an alignment between CCSS and the academic learning goal(s) for instruction. It also provides a place to list the materials needed, cite sources for the content, and identify appropriate technology utilized. The Preliminary Information section informs the other components in the lesson plan.

B. *Lesson Procedures and Differentiation* sections and outlines the how-to section of the lesson plan. This section includes how to introduce the lesson content, key vocabulary, step-by-step instructions for the lesson content, differentiated student activities by language level, and corresponding differentiated instructional products by language level.

C. *Outcomes and Assessment* wrap up the alignment with the CCSS and differentiated instruction. There are two components to this section. The differentiated expected outcomes by language level and the formative assessment tool(s). I use the term "expected outcome" because it is stating a hope for this lesson. In other words, you put in writing what you hope students will gain as a result of this lesson, if all goes according to plan. Stating expected outcomes also predicts the form and content of the formative assessments that are applied to the lesson.

Table 8.2 Differentiated Lesson Plan Format

A. *Preliminary Information*
1. Grade level(s)
2. Performance level(s)
3. Subject area
4. Common Core standard(s)
5. Academic learning goal(s)
6. Materials, resources, technology
B. *Lesson Procedures and Differentiation*
1. Introducing the lesson content
2. Key vocabulary
3. Step-by-step instructions
4. Differentiated student activities and products by performance level
C. *Outcomes and Assessment*
1. Differentiated expected outcomes by language level
2. Formative assessment tool(s)

(See the Differentiated Lesson Plan Template available as an eResource, www.routledge.com/books/details/9781138017696/)

What to Write in Each Part of the Differentiated Lesson Plan

A. Preliminary Information

1. **Grade Level(s)**: Ex: Grade 3
2. **Reading Performance Level(s):** Identify the language level (Performance level 1, 2, or 3—Level 3 is performing at grade level, Level 2 is developing grade-level performance, and Level 1 is undeveloped in English)
3. **Subject Area/Domain:** Ex: Reading/Fluency
4. **Common Core Standard(s):** Write out the entire standard(s) to remind yourself, or the teacher using the plan, what you are aiming for. When only the reference numbers are cited, it is not quite so obvious. Include the title of the standard and the numeric reference for accurate citation, Ex: *CCSS.ELA-LITERACY.RF.3.4.B*
   Read grade-level prose and poetry orally with accuracy, appropriate rate, and expression on successive readings

5. **Academic Learning Goal(s):** The goal supplies specific information about this lesson in alignment with the language of the selected Common Core standard(s), Ex: After learning key vocabulary, the students will practice with a partner, reading the poem, "Autumn" (Dickenson, 1960) with accuracy, appropriate rate, and expression to a small group.

6. **Materials, Resources, Technology:** Include all materials needed for the lesson; provide accurate citation of resources for ready retrieval, and identify the technology employed (digital media, tools, search engines). Ex:
   - *Materials*:
     - A class set of the poem, "Autumn."
     - The poem, "Autumn," written in large letters on a large sheet of paper.
     - Word cards for: Morns, Meeker, Plumper, Scarlet, Gown, Scarf, Maple, Trinket.
     - Pictures of: autumn mornings in different locations, animals and people who look meek, women in scarlet evening gowns, maple trees with red foliage.
     - A collections of: plump berries, scarlet red and brown cloths, maple leaves, small trinkets.
   - *Resource*:
     - Dickinson, E. (1960/1893). Autumn. *The Compete Poems of Emily Dickinson*. Boston: Little, Brown.
   - *Technology*:
     - Google images for pictures.

B. Lesson Procedures and Differentiation

1. **Introducing the Lesson Content:** There are essentially two ways to introduce a lesson: (1) Use an object or a picture to tie the lesson to a shared experience; or (2) Tie the current lesson back to previous learning. Ex:
   - Show a picture of an autumn morning: "Look at this picture of a morning. What time of year do you think it was taken? We call this time of year 'Fall,' and we also call it 'Autumn.' Today we are going to read and practice reading in partners a poem called 'Autumn' by Emily Dickenson. But first, let's learn some words from the poem."

2. **Key Vocabulary:** List and define vocabulary
   - Morns: mornings, for short
   - Meeker: gentle, timid
   - Plumper: fat and curvy

- Scarlet: brilliant red
- Gown: a long formal dress
- Maple: a tree with a large leaf that turns color in autumn
- Scarf: a length of cloth worn around the neck
- Trinket: a small item such as a pin or pendent

3. **Step-by-Step Instructions:** Use verb-driven language to provide clear directions for teaching: Ex:
   - *Vocabulary development*: Show the pictures and have the students handle the objects as you describe each item and related it to the word card.
     - (a) Look at these pictures of autumn mornings. What do you see? Now look at the word mornings. I'm going to make it shorter like our poet, Emily Dickenson. Take out the *-ing* from the word to spell "morns." This is how our poet uses the word for mornings.
     - (b) Look at these faces of people and animals. How do they look? Gentle or timid? The poet calls this "Meek" or even more so, "Meeker."
     - (c) Touch these round berries. Do they look curvy? Do they feel juicy ready to eat? When berries are round and juicy, we call them "Plump," or even more so, "Plumper." Look for the word "plumper" in the poem as you read.
     - (d) Hand out the red and brown strips of cloth. You may know the colors of these cloths. One is brown; the other is a kind of red—a bright and brilliant red. The poet calls it "Scarlet." Can you think of anything else that you've seen that is the color scarlet? We are going to tie these together in a moment.
     - (e) Look at these pictures of fancy women. They are wearing long, fancy dresses. Our poet used the word, "Gown," which is a long, fancy dress. In her poem, she says a "scar-let gown"; but she is not referring to woman's dress—it is a field of red flowers. Use your imagination to picture a field of red flowers that looks like a gown. In a little bit, I'm going to ask you to draw a picture of that field.
     - (f) Pick a leaf from my basket. Hold your hand up to the leaf. Look at the colors of the leaf. This is a leaf from a maple tree. In autumn, maple leaves turn color from green to yellow, orange, and red; and then they turn brown.
     - (g) Take the red and brown cloths now. Tie the ends together to make a scarf. Wrap the scarf around your neck. Imaging that you are a Maple tree with red leaves like the scarf around your neck.

(h)   Look at these pins and things in this box. The word for these tiny objects is "trinkets." Take a trinket and pin it to your scarf. As you read the poem, see what the poet does with trinkets.

4.   **Differentiated Student Activities by Language Level**

(a)   *To all students*: Read the entire poem aloud to students modeling accuracy, rate, and expression. Have the students point to the key vocabulary words as they appear in the poem.

(b)   *Level 1 and 2 ELLs*: Choral reading of the poem with the teacher written a large sheet of paper. The teacher models how to read pointing to the words and highlighting the key vocabulary by matching pictures and objects to each key vocabulary word. In pairs they can practice each reading one line of the poem, taking turns to read a single stanza together.

(c)   *Level 3 and above ELLs*: Choral read the poem one time with the whole group; then divide in pairs to practice reading the first stanza of the poem, taking turns being reader and listener. If they can read one stanza with accuracy, rate, and expression then they can practice the second stanza. When they are ready, they read the stanza(s) aloud to a group of students of any language level.

(d)   *Homework*: Read a stanza or two of the poem "Autumn" to at least three people, such as a parent, an adult, or older brother or sister. Ask each person that you read to sign their name on the paper with the copy of the poem.

5.   **Differentiated Instructional Products by Language Level:** Not every lesson with foundational skills in reading will have a tangible product; but in certain cases the product may be an oral presentation of a skill. Ex:

(a)   Level 1 and 2 ELLs: Read one stanza aloud to a small group with some degree of accuracy, rate, and expression.

(b)   Level 3 and above ELLs: Read one or two stanzas aloud with a high degree of accuracy, rate, and expression.

C. Outcomes and Assessment

1.   **Differentiated Expected Outcomes by Language Level:** Define the outcome(s)

(a)   Language level 1 and 2 will read one stanza of the poem for accuracy, rate, and expression.

(b)   Language level 3 will read two stanzas of the poem for accuracy, rate, and expression.

(c)   Accuracy: Accurate pronunciation of the poem with no errors.
(d)   Rate: Proper pacing and pauses.
(e)   Expression: Fully expressive voice.
2. **Formative Assessment Tool(s):** Select the assessment instrument that matches the academic learning goal and the defined outcomes (see Table 8.3 as an example).

Table 8.3 Fluency Rubric

Fluency	4	3	2	1	Comments
Accuracy	Accurate pronunciation (No errors)	Some words mispronounced (1–4 errors)	Most words mispronounced (5 or more errors)	Multiple errors (10 or more)	
Rate	Proper pacing and pauses	Hesitates to decipher some words	Frequent hesitation to decode most words	Struggles to decode each word	
Expression	Fully expressive voice	Some expression in voice	Little expression in voice	No expression used	
Points (Sum the points in each column)					**Total Points** (Sum the row. Max 12 points)

(The teacher may assess students' fluency levels with the above rubric. It can also be provided to the students to give peer-feedback to their classmates.)

Aligning Common Core Standards to Differentiated Learning and Assessment

A final note about differentiated lesson planning is to recognize at what points Common Core alignment takes place in the template. There are five points in the lesson plan that are pivotal to CCSS alignment. Those five points:

1. Common Core standard(s)
2. Academic learning goal(s)
3. Differentiated student products and activities
4. Differentiated expected outcomes by language level
5. Formative assessment tool(s)

One way to gauge the alignment of your lesson is to scan the above points in the plan itself. Read the standard and compare the language in the standard to the academic learning goal, expected outcomes, and formative assessment. If there is a high degree of connection at these points in the lesson plan, you can be certain that the balance of the plan is well aligned with the Common Core. The academic learning goal states specifically what the lesson will entail in line with the standard. What activity the student is doing is very telling. If the lesson plan cannot clearly articulate what the student is doing, then the teacher is not actively engaging the students in Common Core learning. The outcomes will state the expectation for the learning in brief; and the formative assessment tool will measure those outcomes in alignment with the CCSS.

Scan your own lesson plans in terms of standards, goals, student activities, outcomes, and assessment. If they appear disconnected, then there is little coherence to the plan. However if the plan is well connected across those five points in the plan, there is strong alignment in place.

The final chapter in this book will demonstrate K–5 differentiated lessons for CCSS Reading-Foundational Skills using recommended performance tasks developed by the framers of the Common Core.

References

Boyd-Batstone, P. (2007). *Anecdotal records assessment: An observational tool with a standards-based focus.* Norwood, MA: Christopher Gordon Publishers.

Cervantes, M. (1604/2003). *Don Quixote.* London: Penguin.

Courey, S.J., Tappe, P., Siker, J., & LePage, P. (2013). Improved lesson planning with universal design for learning (UDL). *Teacher Education and Special Education: The Journal of the Teacher Education Division of the Council for Exceptional Children,* 36(1), 7–27.

Dickinson, E. (1960/1893). Autumn. *The Compete Poems of Emily Dickinson.* Boston: Little, Brown.

Goldston, M.J., Day, J.B., Sundberg, C., & Dantzler, J. (2010). Psychometric analysis of a 5E learning cycle lesson plan assessment instrument. *International Journal of Science and Mathematics Education,* 8(4), 633–648.

Grant, C.A., & Sleeter, C.E. (2006). Turning on learning: Five approaches for multicultural teaching plans for race, class, gender and disability. Indianapolis, IN: Jossey-Bass.

John, P.D. (2006). Lesson planning and the student teacher: Rethinking the dominant model. *Journal of Curriculum Studies,* 38(4), 483–498.

McTighe, J., & Thomas, R.S. (February, 2003). Backward Design. *Educational Leadership,* 60(5), 52–55.

9

Differentiated Lesson Plans, K–5

This final chapter of the book brings everything together with sample lesson plans for Kindergarten through 5th grade. They are detailed plans that are ready to use. You may download PDF versions of the plans at www.routledge.com/books/details/9781138017696

Back in Chapter 1, I explained a three-part conceptual approach to teaching ELLs to read. Those three areas are:

Integrated and Interconnected. None of the following lessons teaches Foundational Skills in Reading in an isolated way. I purposefully selected CCSS performance tasks for informational texts in order to integrate foundational skills with other reading tasks. Each lesson interconnects two standards: one from Foundational Skills in Reading and another from Informational Texts in Reading. However, the topics are as varied as the selected texts for reading instruction. As a result, the lessons involve making questions about animals in Kindergarten; learning about the stages of growth with pumpkins in 1st grade; experimenting with bubble surface tension in 2nd grade; using digital tools and music in 3rd grade; space exploration in 4th grade; and understanding the impact of innovation over time with clocks in 5th grade.

Context Supports Complexity. In each lesson, considerable instruction is devoted to building vocabulary and concepts in a context-rich way. This involves using realia, an array of visual images, background music, digital media, and active learning techniques. In the past, conventional reading instruction may not have gone to these lengths to create context-enriched learning environments; but as I hope you have learned from this book, the richer the context for learning, the more meaningful for the student. If it is more meaningful, the ELL will be able to more successfully engage in greater text complexity.

Differentiated Instruction. Each lesson plan is differentiated according Performance Level Descriptors (PLDs). The PLDs are developed for each lesson according to the selected Common Core Standards. The Level 3 PLDs describe grade level performance for a selected standard; Level 2 PLDs describe what approaching grade level performance might look like for that same standard; and Level 1 PLDs describe what to expect if that standard is undeveloped. The range of PLDs was developed with the ELL in mind. They govern the differentiation of activities and instructional products the ELL participate in. They also help define expected learning outcomes for each performance level. Finally, the PLDs define a lesson-specific formative assessment tool to evaluate the performance of students in alignment with CCSS.

Kindergarten CCSS Performance Task

Students ask and answer questions about animals (e.g., hyena, alligator, platypus, scorpion) they encounter in Steve Jenkins and Robin Page's *What Do You Do With a Tail Like This?*

Making Questions About Animal Parts

A. *Preliminary Information*

1. Grade Level(s)

> Kindergarten

2. Performance Level(s)

> 1, 2, & 3

3. Subject Area

> Reading Informational Texts: Phonological Awareness; and Craft and Structure

4. Common Core Standard(s)

> **Phonological Awareness**
> CCSS.ELA-LITERACY.RF.K.2.B
> Count, pronounce, blend, and segment syllables in spoken words.
>
> **Craft and Structure**
> CCSS.ELA-LITERACY.RI.K.4
> With prompting and support, ask and answer questions about unknown
>   words in a text.

5. CCSS Performance Task(s)

> Students ask and answer questions about animals (e.g., hyena, alligator, platypus, scorpion) they encounter in Steve Jenkins and Robin Page's *What Do You Do With a Tail Like This?*

6.   Materials, Resources, Technology

Jenkins, S. & Page, R. (2003). *What Do You Do With a Tail Like This?* Boston: Houghton Mifflin Company.

Multiple sets of picture cards of animal and human noses, ears, tails, eyes, feet, and mouths.

A large clozed sentence strip saying:

What does _____ **do with** _____ **like** _____ **?**

Student worksheets with an exemplar question written completely at the top of the page, three of the clozed sentence frames printed out, and an open space to write a complete question without the frame.

Single sided word cards for each animal name; nose, ears, tail, eyes, feet, mouth.

Double sided word cards for **a/an** on opposite sides and **this/these** on opposite sides.

24 Egg cartons (not made from Styrofoam, but made of pressed cardboard)

Scissors

Paint

Elastic ribbon

B. *Lesson Procedures and Differentiation*

1.   Introducing the Lesson Content

Picture Card Sort

◆   Provide the students with a large array of mixed-up pictures of animal and human noses, ears, tails, eyes, feet, mouths.

◆   Ask students to group the pictures into like groups.

◆   Once the pictures are grouped asked them to select one picture from each group to represent the entire group.

◆   Label each picture group as one of the following word cards: nose, ears, tail, eyes, feet, mouth.

◆   Hold up the representative picture card and word card label.

◆   Ask the question: What do you do with a *nose* like this? (Repeat with another example.)

◆   Say: Today we are going to explore what animals do with these things.

---

2. Key Vocabulary

nose, ears, tail, eyes, feet, mouth

3. Step-by-Step Instructions

Conduct a book walk through *What Do You Do With a Tail Like This?*

◆ Show the cover of the book.
◆ Ask students to point to the title of the book.
◆ Highlight the word "What . . ." as the start of a question.
◆ Highlight the question mark (?) as the ending punctuation of a question.
◆ As you walk through the book, ask the students to point to the text each time a question appears.
◆ Note the slight changes in some words in the question (**a/an**; **this/these**).
◆ As you see each animal part (nose, ears, tail, eyes, feet, mouth) in the text, ask the students to show you with their hands what an animal part is like; for example: Show me a nose like an elephant.
◆ Make explicit that "elephant" has three syllables: el-e-phant.
◆ Ask: What does an elephant do with a nose like this?
◆ Continue with that pattern of showing the animal part, counting the syllables in the animal name, and asking a specific question.

Clozed Sentence Strip

On a large white board display the sentence strip:
What does _____ do with _____ like _____?

◆ Insert an animal word card, an animal part word card.
◆ Ask: What should I use here? (**a** or **an**) . . . flip the two-sided card as you show the possible answers.
◆ Ask: What should I use here? (**this** or **these**) . . . flip the two-sided card as you show the possible answers.
◆ Write in the selected words over each blank space on the white board.
◆ Now let's ask the questions: What does ***an elephant*** do with ***a nose*** like ***this***?
◆ Repeat this pattern of inserting word cards and writing a question.

Now we are going to divide into three table groups:

- **Table 1** will write questions about the animals.
- **Table 2** will read *What Do You Do With a Tail Like This?* with a teacher or teacher helper.
- **Table 3** will make animal parts with egg cartons.

After we finish writing questions and making animal parts, we will play animal questioning mixer where you ask each other "What are you going to do with your nose, ears, tails, eyes, feet, or mouth?"

4. Differentiated Student Activities and Products by Performance Level

Table 1: Write questions about the animals.

- Each child is given a sentence frame worksheet.
- Using the exemplar, teacher prompting, and word cards, students complete three sentence frames.

Level 1 students may complete one to two questions and illustrate them.
Level 2 students may complete three questions and illustrate them.
Level 3 students complete three questions, write their own question without a frame, and illustrate them.

Table 2 will read *What Do You Do With a Tail Like This?* with a teacher or teacher helper.
As the adult reads the book,

- Pause to count the syllables for each animal name.
- Pause to allow students to formulate the questions and find the answers.
- Highlight the component parts of a question in the text.

Level 1 students point to the questions as they appear.
Level 2 students formulate questions according to the format in the book.
Level 3 students may initiate additional questions about the animals.

Table 3 will select an animal part to make from an egg carton.

- Use the egg cartons to make the various animal parts as presented in the text of the book: nose, ears, tail, eyes, feet, mouth.

◆ This is a creative project. For example students can cut out and string together the eggcups from the carton to form an elephant nose.
◆ Cut and splay the ends of an eggcup to make an anteater nose.
◆ Two eggcups can form ears or eyes.
◆ Allow for imaginative creations.
◆ Tie the eggcup animal parts on with elastic ribbon.

Whole Group: Animal Questioning Mixer
Students wear their animal parts created from egg cartons.
Rehearse asking starter questions:

Level 1 (Yes/No answers) Is that a nose? Eyes? Ears? Feet? A Mouth?
Level 2 (Single word answers) What animal are you?
Level 3 (Open ended answers) What does a (INSERT ANIMAL NAME) do with ***a nose*** like that? Eyes? Ears? Feet? A Mouth?

◆ Begin in a small group. Practice asking the questions to each other.
◆ Open up to the entire group.
◆ Play music in the background when they ask each other questions.
◆ Stop the music to signal that the mixer has stopped.
◆ Ask the students what they learned.
◆ Repeat the mixing; but consider moving students around so that everyone is asked a question.

C. *Outcomes and Assessment*

1. Differentiated Expected Outcomes by Performance Level

Level 1 Students

◆ Point to a question in a text.
◆ Clap syllable counts.
◆ Reply to Yes/No questions.
◆ Formulate and illustrate a question.

Level 2 Students

◆ Identify the component parts of a question.
◆ Appropriately clap-out the syllable counts of animal names.

◆ Reply to questions with at least one-word responses.
◆ Formulate questions about animals.

Level 3 Students

◆ Name components of a question including beginning word and ending punctuation.
◆ Count syllables of multi-syllabic words.
◆ Formulate and create questions based on the text of the book.

2. Formative Assessment Tool(s)

CCSS-Kindergarten Foundational Skills/ Informational Texts	Level 1 Undeveloped	Level 2 Approaching grade	Level 3 At grade level
Phonological Awareness	Does not comprehend simple spoken words. Does not distinguish syllables and individual sounds in words.	Isolates and pronounces the initial, medial vowel, and final sounds (phonemes) in three-phoneme (consonant-vowel-consonant, or CVC) words.	Counts, pronounces, blends, and segments syllables in spoken words.
Craft and Structure	Points to unknown words in the text.	Asks, "What does an animal do with a _____ like that?" Makes random guesses about unknown words in the text.	With prompting and support, asks and answers questions about unknown words in a text.

First Grade CCSS Performance Task: Students use the illustrations along with textual details in Wendy Pfeffer's *From Seed to Pumpkin* to describe the key idea of how a pumpkin grows.

Pumpkin Growth Cycle: Stages and Details

A. *Preliminary Information*

1. Grade Level(s)

> 1

2. Performance Level(s)

> 1, 2, & 3

3. Subject Area

> Reading Informational Texts: Print Concepts; and Integration of Knowledge and Ideas

4. Common Core Standard(s)

> **Print Concepts**
>
> CCSS.ELA-LITERACY.RF.1.1.A
> Recognize the distinguishing features of a sentence (e.g., first word, capitalization, ending punctuation).
>
> **Integration of Knowledge and Ideas**
>
> CCSS.ELA-LITERACY.RI.1.7
> Use the illustrations and details in a text to describe its key ideas.

5. CCSS Performance Task(s)

> Students use the illustrations along with textual details in Wendy Pfeffer's *From Seed to Pumpkin* to describe the key idea of how a pumpkin grows.

6.   Materials, Resources, Technology

Pfeffer, W. (2004). *From Seed to Pumpkin*. New York: Harper Collins Children's
    Books.
Video clip (6 minutes): *From Seeds to Pumpkin* read aloud by a child. http://
    youtube/8tZH3W1U9Y4
Video clip (2 minutes): Pumpkins Grow in 85 Days. http://vimeo.com/14019907
Video Clip (7 minutes): Dustin Tate. Growing Pumpkins Time Lapse. http://
    youtube/Pq4kkQQgV88
Video Clip (4 minutes): Matt Radach. Giant Pumpkin Time Lapse.wmv. http://
    youtube/NttZk33LD4A

◆   Six Stages of the Pumpkin Growth Cycle—Worksheet table
◆   Large sheet of white paper cut into a circle (three feet in diameter)
◆   TPR chart with numbered commands (see below)
◆   A pumpkin to slice open
◆   Carving knife
◆   Newspaper
◆   Paper towels
◆   Pocket magnifying glass
◆   Paper for illustrating
◆   Colored markers and crayons
◆   Pictures: seedlings, vines, pumpkin flowers, pumpkin patches
◆   Other realia: dry dirt/fertile soil; broad pumpkin leaves; pumpkin flower

B. *Lesson Procedures and Differentiation*

1.   Introducing the Lesson Content

*(Ideally there would be a garden area for a pumpkin patch at your school with
pumpkin plants already growing. Taking time to explore the actual pumpkin
patch is a perfect use of realia to give context to ELLs.)*

Pumpkin Realia

◆   Layout newspaper on a table in front of the class.
◆   Place a pumpkin on the covered table.
◆   Say: Today we are going to read Wendy Pfeffer's **From Seed to Pumpkin**.
    But first we need to explore where the pumpkin seeds come from.

- ◆ Slice open the pumpkin.
- ◆ Give students a paper towel, and invite them to extract a few seeds.
- ◆ Provide pairs of students with a pocket magnifying glass to examine the seed for details such as colors, shapes, contours, and texture.
- ◆ Encourage them to talk about what they see; what they look like to generate descriptive details in words.
- ◆ Provide them with paper and colored pencils to draw a detailed illustration of a pumpkin seed.

2. Key Vocabulary

NOUNS AND NOUN ADJUNCTS: seed, seedlings, sprout, soil, vine, leaves, flower, pumpkin patch

3. Step-by-Step Instructions

Vocabulary Instruction

After the students have explored pictures or realia from the pumpkin, follow by labeling each item with a word card.

- ◆ **Seedlings and Sprouts:** Show pictures of pumpkin seeds and sprouts. Compare the words SEEDS/SEEDLINGS.
- ◆ **Soil:** Bring in dry dirt and fertile soil. Examine the differences with the students.
- ◆ **Vine:** Show a picture of large pumpkin vine.
- ◆ **Pumpkin Leaves:** Provide big broad pumpkin leaves for students to touch. Notice the jagged edges and prickly hairs on the leaves.
- ◆ **Flower:** Show sample pictures of pumpkin flowers. You might even want to wear a pumpkin flower as a boutonniere or behind your ear.
- ◆ **Pumpkin Patch:** Show pictures of various pumpkin patches.

Read Wendy Pfeffer's *From Seed to Pumpkin*

- ◆ Read aloud the book to the class.
- ◆ Pause at each page to do the following:
- ◆ Identify and highlight key vocabulary
- ◆ Note the components of selected sentences (Word capitalization and ending punctuation).
- ◆ Make reference to the stage of growth.

Ask: What do you see? Where do you see it? What's going on here? What would you call this stage of growth?

Growth Cycle

Take the large paper circle.
Fold it in half to form a semi-circle.
Then fold it into thirds to make six sections:

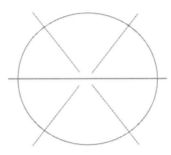

Say: "We are going to recreate the growth cycle of a pumpkin on this large circle. Notice that it has six pie-shaped wedges folded into the paper. In each wedge, we will illustrate and describe in detail the stages of the pumpkins growth cycle."
"First, let's label the stages."
Starting at the top of the circle, write the stage number and descriptor word moving clockwise from wedge to wedge.
Six Stages of Pumpkin Growth Cycle

- ◆ Stage 1: Seed
- ◆ Stage 2: Sprout
- ◆ Stage 3: Vine
- ◆ Stage 4: Flower
- ◆ Stage 5: Green pumpkin
- ◆ Stage 6: Orange pumpkin

Divide the class into six small groups, one for each stage of the pumpkin growth cycle.
Small group directions:

- ◆ Use a copy of the book *From Seed to Pumpkin* and selected video clips (listed above) to explore your group's stage of the growth cycle.

◆ Make detailed illustrations and write details about the growth stage.

◆ Consider size, feel or texture, time or duration, color, and shape to describe the stage.

◆ When you have at least four details with illustrations, bring it to the teacher for review.

◆ Paste details and illustrations in the appropriate wedge on the Pie Chart.

Review the entire Pie Chart with the whole class when it is completed.

4. Differentiated Student Activities and Instructional Products by Performance Level

After students create the large Pie Chart of Stages of Growth, each student will be given a worksheet table to complete with a partner or trio group.

Level 1: Illustrates each stage accurately. May include descriptive words copied from the book or vocabulary word cards.

Level 2: Completes the worksheet table with at least one descriptive detail beginning with a capital letter and ending with a period.

Level 3: Completes the worksheet with 2 or more descriptive details written in complete sentences beginning with a capital letter and ending with a period.

C. *Outcomes and Assessment*

1. Differentiated Expected Outcomes by Performance Level

Level 1 Students

◆ Point to appropriate illustrations of specific details.

◆ Illustrate details about the stages of growth of a pumpkin.

◆ Point to a detail written in the text as a sentence.

◆ Use vocabulary words orally.

Level 2 Students

◆ Identify the initial capital letter and ending punctuation in a sentence.

◆ Use sentences to orally describe details.

◆ Illustrate details about the stages of growth of a pumpkin.

◆ Utilize the key vocabulary in writing details about the growth of a pumpkin.

Level 3 Students

- ◆ Identify the initial capital letter and ending punctuation in a sentence.
- ◆ Write a sentence to describe a detail.
- ◆ Illustrate details about the stages of growth of a pumpkin.
- ◆ Utilize the key vocabulary in writing details about the growth of a pumpkin.

---

2. Formative Assessment Tool(s)

CCSS-Grade 1 Foundational Skills/ Informational Texts	**Level 1** Undeveloped	**Level 2** Approaching grade level	**Level 3** At grade level
Print Concepts	Does not distinguish words as separated by spaces. May not follow words from left to right.	Identifies the first word of a given sentence. Names the capital letters in words. Points out the ending punctuation of sentences.	Recognizes the distinguishing features of a sentence (e.g., first word, capitalization, ending punctuation).
Integration of Knowledge and Ideas	Does not describe key ideas. Only points out illustrations that match details in the text.	Identifies some details found in illustrations and the text. Describes 1–2 key ideas.	Uses the illustrations and details in a text to describe its key ideas.

Six Stages of Pumpkin Growth Cycle			
Stages	Descriptor	Illustration	Details
Stage 1	Seed		
Stage 2	Sprout		
Stage 3	Vine		
Stage 4	Flower		
Stage 5	Green pumpkin		
Stage 6	Orange pumpkin		

Second Grade CCSS Performance Task

Bubble Surface Tension

A. *Preliminary Information*

1. Grade level(s)

> 2

2. Performance level(s)

> 1, 2, and 3

3. Subject Area

> Reading Informational Texts: Phonics and Word Recognition; Integration of Knowledge and Ideas

4. Common Core Standard(s)

> **Phonics and Word Recognition**
>
> CCSS.ELA-LITERACY.RF.2.3.E
> Identify words with inconsistent but common spelling-sound correspondences.
>
> **Integration of Knowledge and Ideas**
>
> CCSS.ELA-LITERACY.RI.2.7
> Explain how specific images (e.g., a diagram showing how a machine works) contribute to and clarify a text.

5. CCSS Performance Task(s)

> Students explain how the specific image of a soap bubble and other accompanying illustrations in Walter Wick's *A Drop of Water: A Book of Science and Wonder* contribute to and clarify their understanding of bubbles and water.

6. Materials, Resources, Technology

Walter Wick, W. (1997). *A Drop of Water: A Book of Science and Wonder.* New York: Scholastic, Inc.

- A balloon
- A round circle of paper
- Paper cups (a class set)
- Eyedroppers (a class set)
- Liquid dish soap
- Bubble rings for blowing bubbles (10 each)
- Metric ruler
- Stop watch
- Bubble Record Sheet (a class set)
- Word cards of key vocabulary

B. *Lesson Procedures and Differentiation*

1. Introducing the Lesson Content

Dip a bubble ring into a cup of soapy water and blow a large bubble.
Repeat the action, only this time, use a clean, dry bubble ring and dip it into clean water.
Ask the class to think about, What is happening here? (Repeat the demonstration.)
Today we are going to read some of Walter Wick's *A Drop of Water: A Book of Science and Wonder*.
We will first learn about some key words; then we will read for information; and then we will experiment with bubbles.

---

2. Key Vocabulary

---

emerging, dazzling, shimmering, breaking, surface tension, precision, bubble, sphere, circle, and collapse

---

3.   Step-by-Step Instructions

Vocabulary, Phonics and Word Recognition

I'm going to show you four words:

> **Emerging**
> **Dazzling**
> **Shimmering**
> **Breaking**

- ◆   How are they alike? (They end in -ing)
- ◆   We use -ing when something is happening or going on now.
- ◆   Watch as I blow a bubble. You will see the bubble "**emerging**" from the bubble ring. Make the motion of a bubble emerging with your hands.
- ◆   Blow a large bubble again.
- ◆   See the colors and light in the bubble? We call that "**dazzling**." How can we show "dazzling" with our hands? Hands open around the eyes.
- ◆   Blow a large bubble again.
- ◆   See how the bubble shakes and quivers in the light? We call that "**shimmering**." Form a bubble shape with your hands, now make them lightly shake and shimmer.
- ◆   Blow a large bubble again until it breaks.
- ◆   What is happening to our bubble? It is **breaking**. Show me with your hands a bubble shape breaking.
- ◆   We are going to use these words to describe bubbles. But review with your hand motions: emerging, dazzling, shimmering, breaking.

Look at these two words:

> **Tension**
> **Precision**

- ◆   How are they alike? (They end in -ion.)
- ◆   Words that end in -ion are very similar in English and in Spanish. When we see -ion at the end of the word, we read it as a description of something, not a verb—or action word.
- ◆   Watch me create **tension**. (Blow up a balloon and then let the air out.)
- ◆   When we stretch the surface of the balloon, we call it "**surface tension**." Notice the shape without surface tension. Now look at the shape with surface tension.
- ◆   **Precision** describes how specifically you can measure something.

◆ Blow up the balloon again. How big is this balloon? Kind of big? Very big? Not so big?

◆ We use precision when we measure. Let the air out of the balloon and measure it across in centimeters.

◆ We are going to use our metric rulers to measure bubbles using centimeters to apply precision.

Now look at this last group of words:

Surface
Bubble
Sphere
Circle
Collapse

◆ How are these words alike? (They all end in a silent-e.)

◆ When we write these words, we include the -e at the end, although we never pronounce the final -e. In English there are many silent consonants, but silent e is a unique vowel. You can't say it, you can't hear it; so you must see it. Oftentimes it changes the way a word sounds, like Sam/Same or Gam/Game. We will use these words to help us describe bubbles too. But each word ends differently than the next, except that the -e is silent.

◆ We've already looked at **surface**, with **surface tension**.

◆ **Bubble** and Balloon are different. Blow up the balloon and then blow up a bubble. How are they different? Bubble = liquid; Balloon = solid.

◆ You almost say the -e at the end of bubble, because of the "ell" sound right before it. Do you hear the /ouhl/ kind of sound?

◆ **Sphere** and **Circle** are different too. Hold up a round cut-out circle, then blow up the balloon again. How are these two different? (Sphere has 3D form; Circle is a flat round shape.)

◆ **Collapse** is a unique word in two parts. Col- means together; -lapse means to slip or fall. So the word means to fall together.

Blow up the balloon. Slowly let out the air so that it collapses into itself. Watch the balloon collapse. Say the word **Col-lapse**.

Review Vocabulary

Get into groups of three students each. Number yourselves 1, 2, or 3.

Student #1: In your own words, hand motions, or drawing, explain the -ing words to the group.

Student #2: In your own words, hand motions, or drawing, explain the -ion words to the group.

Student #3: In your own words, hand motions, or drawing, explain the silent e words to the group.

Reading Walter Wick's *A Drop of Water: A Book of Science and Wonder*

We will do some small group reading together in our groups of three students.

Student #1, read the sentences with vocabulary words ending in -ing.
Student #2, read the sentences with vocabulary words ending in -ion.
Student #3, read the sentences with vocabulary words ending in silent-e.
If you find words in the same sentence, you read it all together. For example look at the first sentence; it has "dazzling," "precision," and "bubble," so you all read it together.
Take a moment to locate your sentences before you begin reading. When you've identified who reads when, you may begin.

Bubble Experiment

(Set up the experiment as follows: two cups, one with water, the other with dish soap; an eyedropper, a bubble ring, a metric ruler, stopwatch, and record sheets (one each for students).
Now that we've learned the vocabulary words and read a selection of the text, we will experiment with bubbles in our small groups of three. We will do the first two rounds of the experiment together.

Round #1

- ◆ Get the stopwatch set, ready to time.
- ◆ Get ready to write and draw on your record sheet.
- ◆ You will record the Bubble life in seconds and measure the bubble size in centimeters; then draw a picture and describe what you saw. Use the key vocabulary words we just learned.

Ready:

- ◆ Dip the bubble ring into the ***clean*** water.
- ◆ Time the bubble and measure it.
- ◆ Blow a bubble, now.
- ◆ Record what you saw.
- ◆ Was it too fast? Try it again.

Round #2

◆ Add two (2) drops of soap to the water.
◆ Dip the bubble ring into the **soapy** water.
◆ Time the bubble and measure it.
◆ To measure, hold the metric ruler across the width of the bubble. If you miss it, try again.
◆ Blow a bubble, now.
◆ Record what you saw.

Round #3

Add four (4) drops of soap to the water.
Repeat the steps and record what you saw.

Round #4

Add eight (8) drops to the water.
Repeat the steps and record what you saw.

Now re-read Walter Wick's *A Drop of Water: A Book of Science and Wonder*, individually or with your small group to understand the concept of **surface tension**.
After re-reading that section, answer the question at the bottom of the record sheet, What's happening here? Talk it over with your group before providing a written response. Try to use some of the vocabulary words in your response.
When you've answered the question, What's happening here? Explain your thinking to another group and compare answers.

4. Differentiated Student Activities and Products by Performance Level

Level 1: Point to key vocabulary in the text and as illustrated in the text. Draws pictures of observations of bubbles. Assists in timing and/or measuring the bubbles.
Level 2: Identifies key vocabulary in the text and uses key words in oral descriptions. Records information in the Bubble record sheet. Assists in timing and/or measuring the bubbles. Orally explains what is happening.
Level 3: Identifies key vocabulary in the text and uses the key words in oral and written descriptions. Records information in the Bubble record sheet. Assists in timing and/or measuring the bubbles. Explains what is happening orally and in writing.

C. Outcomes and Assessment

1. Differentiated Expected Outcomes by Performance Level

Level 1 Students

- ◆ Read along with the other students, might not read aloud as yet.
- ◆ Point to some key vocabulary and relates it to the illustrations.
- ◆ Participate actively in timing and measuring bubbles.
- ◆ Draw observations on the record sheet.

Level 2 Students

- ◆ Point out and reads sentences with key vocabulary in the text.
- ◆ Connect vocabulary to the illustrations in the text.
- ◆ Provide oral descriptions using the key vocabulary.
- ◆ Fully participate in timing, measuring, drawing, and recording observations.
- ◆ Orally explain to others what is happening.

Level 3 Students

- ◆ Identify and read sentences with all key vocabulary in the text.
- ◆ Connect vocabulary to the illustrations in the text.
- ◆ Provide oral and written descriptions using the key vocabulary.
- ◆ Fully participate in timing, measuring, drawing, and recording observations.
- ◆ Explain, orally and in writing to others, what is happening.

---

2. Formative Assessment Tool(s)

CCSS-Grade 2 Foundational Skills/ Informational Texts	Level 1 Undeveloped	Level 2 Approaching grade level	Level 3 At grade level
Phonics and Word Recognition	May identify some key words by pointing.	Identifies some words with inconsistent but common spelling-sound correspondences.	Accurately identifies words with inconsistent but common spelling-sound correspondences.
Integration of Knowledge and Ideas	May point to the appropriate details of an image or diagram identified in the text.	Uses single word or short phrase explanations to explain specific images or diagrams, or to clarify a text.	Explains how specific images contribute to and clarify a text.

Bubble Record Sheet

Drops of soap	Bubble life: Time before burst in seconds	Bubble size In centimeters	Drawings and Descriptions: Vocabulary: dazzling, shimmering, breaking, emerging, surface tension, precision, collapse, bubbles, spheres, and circles
0 drops (no soap)			
2 drops			
4 drops			
8 drops			
What's happening here?			

Third Grade CCSS Performance Task

Students use text features, such as the table of contents and headers, found in Aliki's text *Ah, Music!* to identify relevant sections and locate information relevant to a given topic (e.g., rhythm, instruments, harmony) quickly and efficiently.

Recreating a Table of Contents With Themes and Key Words

A. *Preliminary Information*

1. Grade level(s)

> 3

2. Performance level(s)

> 1, 2, & 3

3. Subject Area

> Reading Informational Texts: Phonics & Word Recognition; Craft and Structure

4. Common Core Standard(s)

> **Phonics and Word Recognition**
>
> CCSS.ELA-LITERACY.RF.3.3.C
> Decode multi-syllable words.
>
> **Craft and Structure**
>
> CCSS.ELA-LITERACY.RI.3.5
> Use text features and search tools (e.g., key words, sidebars, hyperlinks) to locate information relevant to a given topic efficiently.

5. CCSS Performance Task(s)

> Students use text features, such as the table of contents and headers, found in Aliki's text *Ah, Music!* to identify relevant sections and locate information relevant to a given topic (e.g., rhythm, instruments, harmony) quickly and efficiently.

6.   Materials, Resources, Technology

Aliki (2003). *Ah, Music!* New York: Harper Collins Publishers.

Britten, B. Young Person's Guide to the Orchestra—Full length. http://youtube/4vbvhU22uAM

Orchestra: http://en.wikipedia.org/wiki/Orchestra

Tribal Samples, World Percussion Loops, African Rhythms for Download: http://youtube/qmHMj1diooM

Melody loops by Looperman: www.looperman.com/loops/tags/royalty-free-melody-loops-samples-sounds-wavs-download

Harmony loops by Looperman: www.looperman.com/acapellas/tags/harmony-acapellas-vocals-sounds-samples-download

Google docs: Document template with a Table of Contents: https://docs.google.com/previewtemplate?id=1ZwZwIIwCmBa4BiG9IzcD-ZGgW-MXfCcPbSaQwbrIjt8&mode=public

◆   A toy glockenspiel with two (2) mallets to show harmony.
◆   A class set of dry erase whiteboard—lap sized.
◆   A class set of dry erase pens and erasers
◆   Pictures of the following: Ancient Greek orchestra, diagram of a Greek orchestra, diagram of a modern musical orchestra.

B. *Lesson Procedures and Differentiation*

1.   Introducing the Lesson Content

Play the opening movement of Benjamin Britten's "Young Person's Guide to the Orchestra": http://youtube/4vbvhU22uAM

---

2.   Key Vocabulary

Orchestra, instrument, instrumentation, rhythm, melody, harmony.

---

3.   Step-by-Step Instructions

Key Vocabulary, Phonics, and Word Recognition

Provide the students with dry erase lapboards, pens and erasers to write, segment, and analyze multi-syllabic key vocabulary words.

Orchestra: Show photos and diagrams of the ancient Greek orchestra. "Orches-" means to dance or make music and "tra" means place. Put them together you get "orches-tra," a place to make music and dance.

Let's break down the sounds of the word, write the syllable with me:

◆ Or: round your lips and set your jaw to the side to say "or-"
◆ -ches-: make a /k-/ sounds with your breath at the back of your throat; don't buzz; end with an /s-/ sound like a snake—sssss-.
◆ -tra: touch your tongue just behind your teeth, push air out as you open your mouth, and say—ahh. Now put that together, say it,-tra.
◆ How many syllables in Or-ches-tra? (3)
◆ Now say all three in sequence: "Or-ches-tra" again, "orchestra."
◆ Write the word all together on your lapboards, did you come up with eight letters?

Instruments/Instrumentation: Provide each student with a diagram of the orchestra. Return the Benjamin Britten's music video clip http://youtube/4vbvhU22uAM. Play the video and ask the students to point to and identify the various instruments that they see being played.

Compare "instruments" with "instrumentation":

◆ Write both the words on your lapboards.
◆ Underline how the two words alike? *instrument*- and *instrument*-
◆ Circle where they different? -s and -ation
◆ -s means more than one, plural, in this case.
◆ -ation means a group or category.
◆ Say "–a- shun," now say the whole word "instrumentation."

Rhythm: Listen to these African drums play different rhythms: http://youtube/qmHMj1diooM. Rhythms are how musical sounds are organized to flow through time and space. The word is a kind of mash up of the Greek word for rhymes (like sounds) and a river in Germany called the Rhine, which means to flow. Hence sounds flowing.

Let's look at this unique word, rhythm:

◆ There are five consonants and only one vowel.
◆ Say the word "rhythm." How many syllables do you hear? (2)

◆ Smile when you say "rhyth-," spread your lips apart and open your mouth slightly.
◆ Now close your mouth and say /-m/ just like you ate something delicious—mmmmm.
◆ Put it all together to say "rhythm."

Melody: Listen to various melody loops: www.looperman.com/loops/tags/royalty-free-melody-loops-samples-sounds-wavs-download

Melody is a tune, or a phrase of music. Melody combines rhythm and sounds at lower and higher pitches, but it is organized so that it sounds like a unified piece of music. It has a beginning, middle, and end. The word originally meant to speak or pray to a god.
Let's look at the word, melody:

◆ Divide it into syllables: me-lo-dy
◆ Each syllable has a consonant and a vowel. Name each one.
◆ Me- Lips together and drop your jaw to say "me-"
◆ -lo- Lips rounded out; touch your tongue to your front teeth, say "–loh"
◆ -dy: Smile, touch your tongue behind your front teeth, now say "dee"
◆ Put it all together: "Me-lo-dy," again, "Melody"

Harmony: Listen to various harmony loops: www.looperman.com/acapellas/tags/harmony-acapellas-vocals-sounds-samples-download

Harmony in music is the use of more than one pitch or tone at the same time. Demonstrate a simple melodic phrase with one mallet—that's a melody. Demonstrate the phrase—now with two mallets; it's harmony.
Let's look at the word, harmony:

◆ Write the first three letters, har-. Now open your mouth and push air out. Do it again, but this time say—ar with the air. It helps if you move your jaw to one side. Say it again "har-"
◆ Now write the next two letters, -mo-. Put your lips together, then push them out and say "mo-."
◆ Write the last two letters, -ny. Smile with your teeth together; crinkle your nose and say "-ny" like your knee cap.
◆ Write the word together, har-mo-ny. Let's say it together.

Vocabulary Review:

◆ Turn to your seat partner and say these key vocabulary words to each other.
◆ Now pick a word and tell your seat partner what the word means.
◆ Take turns with each key vocabulary word. Use your own words.

Reading Aliki's text *Ah, Music!*

◆ Begin with a quick word search of the text.
◆ Search for the key words we just learned.
◆ When you find a key word, read that sentence to yourself; then read the same sentence again to your partner.
◆ Keep reading until you have found all the key words we just learned.
◆ Write on the dry erase lapboard any multi-syllabic words you had trouble reading.
◆ Now partner read together by alternating sentences or paragraphs.

Create a Table of Contents of Aliki's text, *Ah, Music!* with Key Words

◆ Divide the class into small groups of two to three students.
◆ Divide the text into sections equal to the number of student groups.
◆ Assign a different section of the text to each small group.
◆ Each group must identify the major topics of the section and key words to use in the table of contents.
◆ List the topics in order of the text.
◆ Identify key words to be referenced in each topic.
◆ Include the page numbers that correspond to each topic.
◆ Use Google docs document template to help students create a table of contents from a selection of the text. https://docs.google.com /previewtemplate?id=1ZwZwIIwCmBa4BiG9IzcD-ZGgW -MXfCcPbSaQwbrIjt8&mode=public

4. Differentiated Student Activities and Products by Performance Level

Level 1: Articulates multi-syllabic words with prompting. Partner read with a more proficient reader. First student reads a sentence; second student repeats, reading the same sentence. Helps locate the pages each topic is found in the text. Identifies key words to include in the table of contents.

Level 2: Articulates all key multi-syllabic words accurately. May find other new words in the text. Works with a partner to read and reread the text. Alternates reading sentences with a partner. Produces a complete Table of Contents of their assigned section of the text that includes at least two themes with key vocabulary.

Level 3: Works with a partner alternating reading whole paragraphs. Applies word knowledge to figure out new multi-syllabic words. Produces a complete Table of Contents of their assigned section of the text that includes well defined themes with key vocabulary.

C. *Outcomes and Assessment*

1. Differentiated Expected Outcomes by Performance Level

Level 1 Students

- ◆ Identify key multi-syllabic key words in the text.
- ◆ Formulate and pronounce the syllables of each multi-syllabic word correctly with prompting.
- ◆ Participate in repeated reading with a partner.
- ◆ Help select a topic for the Table of Contents activity.

Level 2 Students

- ◆ Identify and articulate most of the key words in the text.
- ◆ Partner read by alternating sentences.
- ◆ Identify at least two themes in the text.
- ◆ Accurately select key vocabulary for the Table of Contents themes.

Level 3 Students

- ◆ Identify and articulate all appropriate key words in the text.
- ◆ Partner read by alternating paragraphs.
- ◆ Identify three or more themes in the text.
- ◆ Accurately select key vocabulary for the Table of Contents themes.

2. Formative Assessment Tool(s)

CCSS-Grade 3 Foundational Skills/ Informational Texts	Level 1 Undeveloped	Level 2 Approaching grade level	Level 3 At grade level
Phonics and Word Recognition	Points to key words in the text.	Decodes multi-syllabic words with prompting	Accurately decodes multi-syllable words without prompting.
Craft and Structure	Randomly picks words to locate information. Does not appear to be searching for specific information.	Skims for key words, but may need prompting to identify a topic in the text. Locates a mixture of relevant and off topic information.	Uses text features and search tools (e.g., key words, sidebars, hyperlinks) to locate information relevant to a given topic efficiently.
Table of Contents (TOC)	TOC includes some topics or words from the text.	TOC follows the order of the text, but might have a missing part or gap. TOC includes 2 or more topics accurately listed from the text. Each topic references 1–2 key words found in the text.	The Table of Contents (TOC) follows the order of the text. TOC includes 3 or more topics accurately listed from the text. Each topic references key words found in the text.

Fourth Grade CCSS Performance Task

Students explain how Melvin Berger uses reasons and evidence in his book *Discovering Mars: The Amazing Story of the Red Planet* to support particular points regarding the topology of the planet.

The Red Planet

A. *Preliminary Information*

1. Grade Level(s)

> 4

2. Foundational Skills Level(s)

> 1, 2, & 3

3. Subject Area

> Reading Informational Texts: Phonics and Word Recognition; Craft and Structure

4. Common Core Standard(s)

> **Fluency**
>
> CCSS.ELA-LITERACY.RF.4.4.A
> Read grade-level text with purpose and understanding.
>
> **Integration of Knowledge and Ideas**
>
> CCSS.ELA-LITERACY.RI.4.8
> Explain how an author uses reasons and evidence to support particular
>   points in a text.

5. CCSS Performance Task(s)

> Students explain how Melvin Berger uses reasons and evidence in his book
> *Discovering Mars: The Amazing Story of the Red Planet* to support particular
> points regarding the topology of the planet.

6.   Materials, Resources, Technology

> Berger, M. (1992). *Discovering Mars: The Amazing Story of the Red Planet*. New York: Scholastic.
> Audio file of Gustav Holst's *The Planets: Mars the Bringer of War*. http://en.wikipedia.org/wiki/File:Holst-_mars.ogg PD-USGov-Congress
> Jet Propulsion Laboratory—Mars Science Center. http://mars.jpl.nasa.gov/msl/
> Sample Prezi by Jordan Caskey. Mars the Great Red Planet. http://prezi.com/tjjqidrdipg5/?utm_campaign=share&utm_medium=copy&rc=ex0share
> Pictures: Mars, God of War; the Red Planet
> 3D glasses template: http://mars.jpl.nasa.gov/mars3d/documents/3d_glasses_template.pdf
> Red and blue cellophane
> Glue
> Scissors

B. *Lesson Procedures and Differentiation*

1.   Introducing the Lesson Content

> Start the reading lesson in the school's computer lab.
> To help create ambience and context, as students are getting settled in to the lab and logging on to computers, play an audio file of Gustav Holst's *The Planets: Mars the Bringer of War* (cited above)
> Ask students to log on to Jet Propulsion Laboratory—Mars Science Center. http://mars.jpl.nasa.gov/msl/
> Guide the students through the menu options on the website.
> Ask them to search for the following:
>
> ◆   Information new to you about Mars;
> ◆   Mars in the news—What's happening on Mars?
> ◆   Graphics or videos about Mars;
> ◆   Information or graphics about volcanoes on Mars.
>
> Allow the students 10 minutes to explore the website to find answers.
> Ask selected students to present, for the whole class, the facts and graphics that they found about Mars.
> Say: "Now we are going to read a selection about volcanoes by Melvin Berger, *Discovering Mars: The Amazing Story of the Red Planet*."

2. Key Vocabulary

Mars, Red Planet, surface, mammoth volcanoes, mount/mons

3. Step-by-Step Instructions

Vocabulary Development

Mars: The Greek god of war. Show pictures of Classical and recent representations of the god. Explain that a number of the planets are named after Greek or Roman gods and goddess, such as Jupiter, Venus, and Saturn.

Red Planet: Show selected images of Mars the Red planet from the Jet Propulsion Laboratory website. (http://mars.jpl.nasa.gov/msl/)

Surface: Use 3D glasses to view images of the Martian landscape. (http://mars.jpl.nasa.gov/mars3d/)

Mammoth Volcanoes: Use Google images site to view mammoth volcanoes on Earth and Mars.

Mount/Mons: English/French renderings for the word mountain. Each volcano is referred to as Mount or Mons; like Mount Olympus or Mons Olympus.

Reading: Melvin Berger's *Discovering Mars: The Amazing Story of the Red Planet*

Three options for reading the text:

Option #1: You can sit with the teacher and follow along as the teacher reads aloud.

Option#2: Buddy read with a partner. Take turn reading paragraphs.

Option#3: Read on your own.

Read for the following purposes:

◆ Find four information points about volcanoes on Mars.
◆ Cite each point of information.
◆ Record supporting data to each of the points.
◆ Search the JPL website to find supporting evidence and supporting images.

Use the attached file document as an Information and Evidence Worksheet.

Digital Media Presentation:

View the Sample Prezi by Jordan Caskey. Mars the Great Red Planet.

Work with a team of two to four members to make a digital presentation of the information you uncovered.

Use PowerPoint, Prezi, or Flash.
The presentation must include the following:

- ◆ Three to four points of information.
- ◆ Supporting evidence for each point of information.
- ◆ Accompanying images to support the information.
- ◆ Citation of the information.

4. Differentiated Student Activities and Products by Performance Level

Level 1: Meets with the teacher to listen as the text is read aloud. Contribute to the Information and Evidence Worksheet with the group. Contributes to a collaborative digital presentation.

Level 2: Works with a partner to read the text. Together they complete the Information and Evidence Worksheet. Either continues working with the partner or joins with a team of up to four students to create the digital presentation of Mars.

Level 3: Can work with a partner or individually to read and complete the table, except for the final row about results. Must meet with two to four other students to discuss and justify their thinking about the results.

C. *Outcomes and Assessment*

1. Differentiated Expected Outcomes by Performance Level

Level 1 Students

- ◆ Read with prompting and assistance.
- ◆ Contribute some information to the group.
- ◆ Contribute assistance with the development of the digital presentation.

Level 2 Students

- ◆ Read to find specific information about Mars.
- ◆ Complete the evidence worksheet with assistance from peers and teacher.
- ◆ Synthesize information accurately in the digital presentation.
- ◆ Select and include appropriate and interesting graphics in the digital presentation.

Level 3 Students

◆ Read to find specific information about Mars from multiple sources.
◆ Complete the evidence worksheet accurately.
◆ Synthesize information accurately in the digital presentation.
◆ Select and include appropriate and interesting graphics in the digital presentation.

---

2.   Formative Assessment Tool(s)

CCSS-Grade 4 Foundational Skills/ Informational Texts/ Digital Media	**Level 1** Undeveloped	**Level 2** Approaching grade level	**Level 3** At grade level
Phonics and Word Recognition	Finds random facts about the topic.	Pursues and finds appropriate information with search tools.	Reads grade-level text with purpose and understanding.
Integration of Knowledge and Ideas	Does not identify supporting evidence of the author's points in a text.	Identifies some supporting evidence of the author's points in a text.	Explains how an author uses reasons and evidence to support particular points in a text.
Presentation With Digital Media (Power Point, Flash, or Prezi)	Attempts to employ key vocabulary. Supports an informational point. The presentation is virtually all graphics-based.	Some key vocabulary is included. Some informational points are supported by the text of the presentation. Some informative graphics.	Utilizes all key vocabulary accurately. Information is well-supported in the text of the presentation. Graphics support each point in text.

Information and Evidence Worksheet

Information	Citation	Thumbnail image	Supporting evidence
(1)			
(2)			
(3)			
(4)			

Fifth Grade CCSS Performance Task

Students explain the relationship between time and clocks using specific information drawn from Bruce Koscielniak's *About Time: A First Look at Time and Clocks*.

Clocks and Innovation Over Time

A. *Preliminary Information*

    1.   Grade Level(s)

> 5

    2.   Performance Level(s)

> 1, 2, & 3

    3.   Subject Area

> Reading Informational Texts: Fluency; and Craft and Structure

    4.   Common Core Standard(s)

> **Fluency**
>
> CCSS.ELA-LITERACY.RF.5.4.C
> Use context to confirm or self-correct word recognition and understanding, rereading as necessary.
>
> **Key Ideas and Details**
>
> CCSS.ELA-LITERACY.RI.5.3
> Explain the relationships or interactions between two or more individuals, events, ideas, or concepts in a historical, scientific, or technical text based on specific information in the text.

    5.   CCSS Performance Task(s)

> Students explain the relationship between time and clocks using specific information drawn from Bruce Koscielniak's *About Time: A First Look at Time and Clocks*.

6.   Materials, Resources, Technology

Koscielniak, B. (2004). *About Time: A First Look at Time and Clocks*. Boston: Houghton Mifflin Harcourt Publishing Company.

Pictures: old grandfather clock (inside mechanism and exterior), pocket and wrist watches (inside mechanism and exterior)

Large comparison chart of clocks and portable watches.

Video Clip (1:50 minutes). Ken Kuo. Twin Pivot Grasshopper Escapement— Invented by John Harrison. http://youtube/_VdpRTKGBww

Video Clip (8 seconds). Indexing mechanism. http://youtube/0bRevPdhEco

An 1"×18" strip of sheet metal. (Available for free from the scrap drawer at the local hardware store.)

A ¾"×6" piece of wood dowelling (Available for free from the scrap drawer at the local hardware store.)

A picture of a coiled snake ready to attack.

"Clocks and Time Table" worksheets (a class set—see attachment)

B. *Lesson Procedures and Differentiation*

1.   Introducing the Lesson Content

(*Ideally, if you could show the inside mechanism of a an old wall clock and that of a watch, you would increase the level of comprehension.*)

Show pictures of the interior mechanisms and exterior of old grandfather clocks. Note the pull weights mechanism that relied on gravity to advance the hands of the clock.

Show a short video clip of the "Twin Pivot Grasshopper Escapement" mechanism. Again note the role of gravity to advance the hands.

Show pictures of the interior mechanisms of pocket watches and wrist watches. Note the spiral flat spring mechanism.

Show a short video clip of the flat spring "Indexing Mechanism."

Say: "Today we are going to read Bruce Koscielniak's *About Time: A First Look at Time and Clocks* and examine the relationship between innovation over time and clocks."

2.   Key Vocabulary

flat metal spring, coil, escapement, unwind, gear tooth, portable, watch/watchmen

3.   Step-by-Step Instructions

Vocabulary Development

Flat metal spring: Take a strip of metal and wind it around a piece of wooden dowelling. Refer to the indexing mechanism in the video clip for a visual.

Coil: Show the shape of the flat metal spring. Show a picture of a snake coiled, ready to spring.

Unwind: Show the metal strip as it unwinds.

Gear tooth: Return to a picture of the wall clock mechanism and note the various gears with protruding teeth.

Escapement: The mechanism that generates the pulse for the clock or watch as viewed in the videos.

Origin of the term **watch:** portable clocks were first used by security guards called "Watchmen," hence the term "Watch" or wrist watch.

Reading Bruce Koscielniak's *About Time: A First Look at Time and Clocks*

Begin by orienting the class to what they are about to read.

- ◆   History of clocks.
- ◆   The text begins with a period of time over 500 years ago.
- ◆   It covers a span of approximately 100 years and several European countries including Italy and Germany.

Read and reread the text for the following purposes:

- ◆   Note when events took place;
- ◆   Find the location of the events;
- ◆   Discover who was involved;
- ◆   Identify what was the innovation;
- ◆   Consider the results of the innovations.

Use the "Clocks and Time Information Table" to help you find information. If you can't find the information in the text, leave the space blank.

If you need help reading the text, join the teacher at the small group table. We will read the text aloud and work through the "Clocks and Time Information Table" together.

Be prepared to share the results of these innovations with the whole group. Justify your thinking based on information found in the text.

4. Differentiated Student Activities and Products by Performance Level

Level 1: Meets with the teacher to listen as the text is read and reread aloud. They point out details in the text that pertain to specific time periods.

Level 2: Works with a partner to read and reread the text. Uses context to figure out the meaning of some words. Completes the "Clocks and Time Information Table" with a partner with the exception of the results section. Meets with two to four other students to discuss and justify their thinking about the results.

Level 3: Can work with a partner or individually to read and complete the table, except for the final row about results. Must meet with two to four other students to discuss and justify their thinking about the results.

C. Outcomes and Assessment

1. Differentiated Expected Outcomes by Performance Level

Level 1 Students

◆ Listen with comprehension of key vocabulary as the teacher reads the text aloud.
◆ Point to appropriate illustrations of specific details.
◆ Illustrate details about the innovations.
◆ Point to a written detail in the text within a time period.
◆ Use vocabulary words orally.

Level 2 Students

◆ Read and reread the selected text with purpose.
◆ Use context clues to understand new terms in the text.
◆ Use sentences to orally describe details.
◆ Justify thinking about results of innovations over time.
◆ Utilize some key vocabulary in writing to complete the comparison table.

Level 3 Students

◆ Read and reread the selected text with purpose.
◆ Use context clues to understand new terms in the text.
◆ Use sentences to orally describe details.
◆ Justify thinking about four or more results of innovations over time.
◆ Accurately apply the key vocabulary in writing to complete the comparison table.

2. Formative Assessment Tool(s)

CCSS-Grade 5 Foundational Skills/ Informational Texts	**Level 1** Undeveloped	**Level 2** Approaching grade level	**Level 3** At grade level
Fluency	Does not recognize or understand words that require self-correction. Skips over difficult passages in the text.	Uses context to confirm some word recognition. May neglect to reread or self-correct as necessary.	Uses context to confirm or self-correct word recognition and understanding, rereading as necessary.
Key Ideas and Details	May be able to compare two illustrations of individuals, or events. Struggles to compare abstract ideas or concepts in the text.	With supporting tools, such as a comparison table, is able to explain the relationships between two or more individuals, events, ideas, or concepts based on specific information in the text.	Explains the relationships or interactions between two or more individuals, events, ideas, or concepts in a historical, scientific, or technical text based on specific information in the text.

Clocks and Time Information Table

Clocks/Time	1440	1480	1510	1550
Location				
Inventor				
Innovation				
Results				

Appendix

Sample Lesson Plan

 Differentiated Lesson Plan Using the Template

A. *Preliminary Information*

1. Grade level(s)

> 3

2. Reading Performance level(s)

> Levels 1, 2, and 3

3. Subject Area/Domain

> Reading/Fluency

4. Common Core Standard(s)

> *CCSS.ELA-LITERACY.RF.3.4.B*
> *Read grade-level prose and poetry orally with accuracy, appropriate rate, and expression on successive readings*

5. Academic Learning Goal(s)

> After learning key vocabulary, the students will practice with a partner reading the poem, "Autumn" (Dickinson, 1960) with accuracy, appropriate rate, and expression.

6. Materials, Resources, Technology

> ◆ *Materials*:
> - A class set of the poem, "Autumn."
> - The poem "Autumn," written in large letters on a large sheet of paper.
> - Word cards for: Morns, Meeker, Plumper, Scarlet, Gown, Scarf, Maple, Trinket.
> - Pictures of: Autumn mornings in different locations, Animals and people who look meek, Women in scarlet evening gowns, Maple trees with red foliage.
> - A collections of: Plump berries, Scarlet red and brown cloths, Maple leaves, Small trinkets.
>
> ◆ *Resource*:
> - Dickinson, E. (1960/1893). Autumn. *The Compete Poems of Emily Dickinson*. Boston: Little, Brown.
>
> ◆ *Technology*:
> - Google images for pictures

B. *Lesson Procedures and Differentiation*

1. Introducing the lesson content

> Show a picture of an autumn morning: "Look at this picture of a morning. What time of year do you think it was taken? We call this time of year 'Fall,' and we call it 'Autumn.' Today we are going to read and practice reading in partners a poem called "Autumn" by Emily Dickinson. But first, let's learn some words from the poem."

2. Key vocabulary

> **Key vocabulary**: List and define vocabulary
>
> ◆ Morns: mornings for short
> ◆ Meeker: gentle, timid
> ◆ Plumper: fat and curvy
> ◆ Scarlet: brilliant red
> ◆ Gown: a long formal dress

- ◆ Maple: a tree with a large leaf that turns color in autumn
- ◆ Scarf: a length of cloth worn around the neck
- ◆ Trinket: a small item such as a pin or pendent

3. Step-by-Step Instructions

Vocabulary Development: Show the pictures and have the students handle the objects as you describe each item and relate it to the word card.

a) Look at these pictures of autumn mornings. What do you see? Now look at the word "mornings." I'm going to make it shorter like our poet, Emily Dickinson. Take out the *-ing* from the word to spell "morns." This is how our poet uses the word for mornings.

b) Look at these faces of people and animals. How do they look? Gentle or timid? The poet calls this "Meek" or even more so, "Meeker."

c) Touch these round berries. Do they look curvy? Do they feel juicy—ready to eat? When berries are round and juicy, we call them "Plump," or even more so, "Plumper." Look for the word "plumper" in the poem as you read.

d) Hand out the red and brown strips of cloth. You may know the colors of these cloths. One is brown; the other is a kind of red—a bright and brilliant red. The poet calls it "scarlet." Can you think of anything else that you've seen that is the color scarlet? We are going to tie these together in a moment.

e) Look at these pictures of fancy women. They are wearing long, fancy dresses. Our poet used the word, "gown," which is a long, fancy dress. In her poem, she says a "scarlet gown"; but she is not referring to woman's dress—it is a field of red flowers. Use your imagination and picture a field of red flowers that looks like a gown. In a little bit, I'm going to ask you to draw a picture of that field.

f) Pick a leaf from my basket. Hold your hand up to the leaf. Look at the colors of the leaf. This is a leaf from a maple tree. In autumn, maple leaves turn color from green to yellow, orange, and red; and then they turn brown.

> g) Take the red and brown cloths now. Tie the ends together to make a scarf. Wrap the scarf around your neck. Imaging that you are a maple tree with red leaves like the scarf around your neck.
>
> h) Look at these pins and things in my box. The word for these tiny objects is "trinkets." Take a trinket and pin it to your scarf. As you read the poem, see what the poet does with trinkets.

4.   Differentiated Student Activities and Products by Performance Level

> ◆   *To all students*: Read the entire poem aloud to students modeling accuracy, rate, and expression. Have the students point to the key vocabulary words as they appear in the poem.
> ◆   *Level 1 and 2 ELLs*: Choral reading of the poem with the teacher written on a large sheet of paper. The teacher models how to read pointing to the words and highlighting the key vocabulary by matching pictures and objects to each key vocabulary word. In pairs they can practice each reading one line of the poem, taking turns to read a single stanza together.
> ◆   *Level 3 and above ELLs*: Choral read the poem one time with the whole group; then divide in pairs to practice reading the first stanza of the poem, taking turns being reader and listener. If they can read one stanza with accuracy, rate, and expression; then they can practice the second stanza. When they are ready, they read the stanza(s) aloud to a group of students of any language level.
> ◆   Homework: Read a stanza or two of the poem "Autumn" to at least three people, such as a parent, an adult, or older brother or sister. Ask each person that you read to sign their name on the paper with the copy of the poem.

C.   *Outcomes and Assessment*

1.   Differentiated-Expected Outcomes by Performance Level

> ◆   Language level 1 and 2 will read one stanza of the poem for accuracy, rate, and expression.
> ◆   Language level 3 will read two stanzas of the poem for accuracy, rate, and expression.

> ◆ Accuracy: Accurate pronunciation of the poem with no errors.
> ◆ Rate: Proper pacing and pauses.
> ◆ Expression: Fully expressive voice.

2. Formative Assessment tool(s)

Fluency Rubric

Fluency	4	3	2	1	Comments
Accuracy	Accurate pronunciation (No errors)	Some words mispronounced (1–4 errors)	Most words mispronounced (5 or more errors)	Multiple errors (10 or more)	
Rate	Proper pacing and pauses	Hesitates to decipher some words	Frequent hesitation to decode most words	Struggles to decode each word	
Expression	Fully expressive voice	Some expression in voice	Little expression in voice	No expression used